A Native of Nowhere

A Native of Nowhere
The Life of Nat Nakasa

Ryan Brown

First published by Jacana Media (Pty) Ltd in 2013

10 Orange Street
Sunnyside
Auckland Park 2092
South Africa
+2711 628 3200
www.jacana.co.za

© Ryan Brown, 2013

All rights reserved.

ISBN 978-1-4314-0534-3

Cover design publicide
Set in Ehrhardt 12/16pt
Printed by Ultra Litho (Pty) Ltd, Johannesburg
Job No. 002049

See a complete list of Jacana titles at www.jacana.co.za

For the Nakasa family, who have taught me more about South Africa past and present than anyone else

Contents

Introduction ix
One 1
Two 38
Three 63
Four 77
Five 91
Six 126
Seven 131
Conclusion 164
Notes 174
Acknowledgements 202
Index 208

Introduction

ON A WARM JULY MORNING IN 1965, the South African writer Nat Nakasa stood facing the window of a friend's seventh-floor apartment in Central Park West. In the distance he could likely just make out the outline of the Empire State Building, a sharp reminder of just how far he was from home. Less than a year earlier, Nat had taken an 'exit permit' from the apartheid government – a one-way ticket out of the country of his birth – and come to Harvard University on a journalism fellowship. Now he was caught in a precarious limbo, unable to return to South Africa but lacking citizenship in the United States, a place that he was beginning to feel offered little respite from the brutal racism of his own country. He was, he wrote, a 'native of nowhere ... a stateless man [and] a permanent wanderer', and he was running out of hope.[1] Standing in that New York City apartment building, he faced the alien city. The next thing anyone knew, he was lying on the pavement below. He was 28 years old.

Nat's death stunned a wide circle of writers and artists

in South Africa and the United States. The musician Hugh Masekela, who attended the young journalist's funeral, remembered the event as seminal in his own exile experience, the moment when he first had 'the realisation that we all might die overseas'.[2] Particularly jarring to Hugh and others close to Nat was that his death came on the heels of a brisk and markedly successful career. In the decade preceding his suicide, he had risen to become a senior writer for South Africa's most circulated black news magazine, served as the first black columnist at a prominent white newspaper, and founded a literary journal to showcase African writing. By the time he was in his mid-twenties, he had been published in the *New York Times* and offered a scholarship to hone his craft in the Ivy League. But as for so many South Africans of his generation, leaving his homeland was not simply a matter of deciding to go. It was also a matter of deciding never to come back. Not yet 30 years old, Nat had to look into his future and decide that being legally barred from his homeland was a price worth paying to see the world beyond its borders.

This book tells the story of that short life. In doing so, it seeks in part to answer the troubling question of how Nat found himself in that New York City window in July 1965, desperate to the point of no return. But life, like history, cannot be read backwards, and so any biography of Nat Nakasa must begin with the acknowledgement that he was no simple martyr, no fallen hero of the anti-apartheid cause, but rather an ambitious, talented and flawed man whose life had the cold fortune of colliding with one of the most racially repressive regimes in the modern world.

A Native of Nowhere

At its most basic level, this book tells the story of how a quiet, serious African boy growing up in the sleepy coastal city of Durban in the 1940s became part of the generation of outspoken black South African journalists in the 1950s and 1960s who challenged state-sponsored segregation in that way that only writers can, simply by keeping a detailed record of its existence. In doing so, this story provides an alternative way of thinking about early resistance to apartheid, loosing it from the bonds of the organised opposition movement. For a man like Nat, freedom was not the end point of a long struggle arching toward justice. Rather it was something you took for yourself, day in and day out – one conversation, one interview, one multiracial party at a time.

Moving in a world where liberation and personal ambition were tightly bound, he spent his life seizing news stories, women and literary prestige in South Africa simply because as a talented and educated man, he saw no reason why he should not have them. He did not live on the perch of rigid principle, but rather with the seemingly endless confidence of someone who thought everything he wanted should be his, oppression and racism be damned. That way of thinking pushed him through mid-twentieth-century South Africa on a path as winding and riddled with contradictions as that of the country itself. And ultimately, it led him to the damning choice to leave it all behind.

But more than that perhaps, Nat Nakasa's story is a story of what happens when a human life, small and short and ordinary, finds itself placed against the backdrop of a tumultuous period in history, a period of brutal racism and state-sponsored discrimination, a period that forced hard choices and courageous actions. Nat's life was forever knotted to the reality that he was a black man in twentieth-century South Africa, a fact that no rebellion, no blithe disregard for the system, could ever eliminate. And that larger story is one shot through with betrayal, a tale of dispossessed dreams and downward mobility of the kind that stalked so many black lives in apartheid South Africa.

In the 1930s, Nat's father was a writer who brushed shoulders with Durban's liberal elite and sent his children to private mission schools to groom them for a middle-class future. Those children came of age, however, at a moment when South Africa's long history of segregation was beginning to cohere into a more systematic and meticulous brand of racial hierarchy. The two, including Nat, who managed to go abroad to continue their education did not survive exile, and the other three scattered across the black townships of South Africa, their prospects increasingly dictated by race and poverty. By the time I met Nat's sister, Gladys, his only surviving sibling, in 2011, she occupied a rumpled two-room government-issued house on the outer edge of a Durban township. As an icy twilight descended over the unheated home, she showed me the mat her son laid out on the concrete floor to sleep on each night. 'We waited many years for this place,' she said.

To be sure, then, this is also a story of the scars that apartheid left on those it touched, and in particular on one young journalist with ambitions taller than his race was allowed. But oppression, however terrible, is never all there is to a person's existence. Indeed, for all of the boundaries apartheid created and for all the suffering it wrought, we must never forget that it is not the only plotline in South African history. It is only a piece of the bigger story we all tell about ourselves and the world we inhabit. For Nat, as for every black South African, the system failed time and time again to stop the persistent march of ordinary life, full of personal dreams and family dramas and heartsick love affairs. In this way, telling Nat's story pushes back against what the writer Jacob Dlamini has called 'the fiction that all black South Africans lived, suffered, and struggled the same way against apartheid'.[3] If that were true, as he rightly notes, any black person could stand in for all black people in telling the stories of South African history. But Nat Nakasa is not Nelson Mandela. He is not Steve Biko and he is not Oliver Tambo. His life is built from its own particulars. Its sensibility, its stories, its ending, are all its own.

Americans who study South Africa must all at some point or other contend with a simple question: why? What is it that pulls us to this distant country at the bottom of the world? I found my answer on a cool autumn night in 2010, as I was walking across the campus of the University of North Carolina with Hugh Masekela. 'Did Nat ever speak to you about his mother?' I asked him suddenly. She was a frail woman who had spent most of his childhood severely mentally ill and I was intensely curious about her.

'No,' Hugh said tersely. 'We didn't have that kind of relationship.'

'Because she was in a mental hospital when he was a child and I just wondered—'

'Look,' he interrupted, suddenly animated. 'South Africa itself was a mental hospital back then. It's remarkable anyone survived it.'

As I listened to the interview much later, I found myself latching onto his description of South Africa. The more time I spent rooting around in Nat's world, the more Hugh's description felt like a succinct explanation for what intrigued me about the country's history: apartheid South Africa was, indeed, a kind of mental hospital, barred and closed to the world, its actions governed by an inscrutable kind of logic that you had to be inside of to understand.

I thought of a story told to me by a colleague of Nat's at *Drum*. One day in the 1960s, she said, she drove to a Johannesburg police station to see a friend who had been jailed for his writing. When she knocked at the front door to the building, a gruff Afrikaner policeman opened it and told her that no, she could not enter there. This door was for whites only. Where then, she asked, should she go? He pointed to the next door, identical to the one she was standing at and not three feet away from it, leading to the same foyer. She sidestepped over, knocked at the second door, and the same policeman opened it and ushered her inside.[4]

Here was a country unhinged by its own obsession with difference, a place that for decades resisted the undertow of anti-colonialism pulling the rest of the continent toward African majority rule. I will not be the first or the last foreigner to say that the spooky singularity of modern South

A Native of Nowhere

African history hooked me. Poised at the intersection of richly cosmopolitan and maddeningly parochial, South Africa was a stubborn pariah state with a white-knuckled grip on its own version of reality. For decades it was a bogeyman of global politics – and with good reason. As late as the 1990s, many public amenities were segregated and most black South Africans were still barred from living on the vast majority of their own nation's land.

When I moved to South Africa in 2011, I found that that history had a visceral presence in the contemporary country. In the city of Johannesburg one can pass in ten minutes' time from the richest square mile on the African continent to a shack settlement without running water. The average income of black South Africans is just 13 per cent that of whites, and since the country's first democratic elections in 1994, the gap between the rich and the poor has actually grown wider, making it perhaps the most unequal society in the world. It is a place where there is no skirting history, because it is on raw and constant display in the present. Look, South Africa seems to be saying to its visitors, our past is no museum exhibit. It cannot be held at a distance, hidden behind glass, never touched. Instead, it crashes straight into the present, leaving deep grooves in the world around us.

Perhaps nowhere is this point more evident than in the leadership of South Africa today. Since 1994, most of those who have governed the country earned their post, directly or indirectly, through their credentials in 'the struggle'. Indeed, all four of the country's post-1994 presidents, Nelson Mandela, Thabo Mbeki, Kgalema Motlanthe and the sitting head of state, Jacob Zuma, came to that office with personal histories that stretch back through the era of apartheid. All were prominent freedom fighters for the African National Congress (ANC) during the long decades of the struggle for democracy. They arrived at their nation's highest governmental post carrying the complex and not easily discernible weight of that history with them, and it has coloured both the way they govern and their broader vision for South Africa.

In particular, as the ANC moved from being a freedom movement to the far less coherent task of ruling a nation, its leaders reached back into the tumultuous history behind them for a past that would lead neatly to their present. A new nation needed a new nationalism, and a new nationalism needed its own founding fathers. 'As you are aware,' President Mbeki told delegates of the Organisation of African Unity in 1999, 'the movement of our own struggle for national liberation is the ANC, the African National Congress.' The country, he continued, had been 'brought up ... by this movement and led by it'.[5] But with the ANC celebrating its hundredth anniversary in 2012 and approaching two decades in control of the South African government, it has become all the more important to complicate its telling of the country's story, and to be always mindful of that fundamental truth about history: there is no objective version of the past. There are only the versions we mould, casting and recasting them again and again to meet the needs of the present.

Indeed, as we speed away from apartheid, it becomes ever easier to see it as a land of stark moral dichotomies – oppressor and oppressed, resister and accomplice, black and

A Native of Nowhere

white. After all, during apartheid South Africa engaged in discrimination so caricatured and vicious that it came to serve as a kind of global moral battleground, posing questions about injustice and inequality that reached far beyond its borders. 'What made [South Africa] different from other gripping lands and absorbing conflicts was its many ways of looking at itself: of explaining, rationalizing, and forgetting,' wrote Joseph Lelyveld, an American journalist who served as a *New York Times* correspondent in South Africa in the 1960s and 1980s.[6] Indeed, few nations, few societies, have grappled so painfully for so long with questions of race, inequality and discrimination as South Africa has.

But despite the obvious drama of this story, South African history is more complicated than this narrative lets on, its endings far less neat and inevitable. It was not predetermined, for instance, that a boy growing up in a crowded, violent township outside Durban in the 1940s would become a resistance fighter, for while this was Jacob Zuma's story, it was Nat Nakasa's as well. Drinking and writing poetry with Johannesburg intellectuals in the late 1950s could turn you into a writer, as it did Nat, or an activist, as it did Thabo Mbeki. Nat, Mandela and Mbeki were all part of the same educated, middle-class minority of Africans who watched apartheid shift into place over the course of their childhood and young adult years, casting a shadow over what had once been a relatively open future for those of their social class. But while that experience propelled all three into a lifelong resistance to apartheid, they did not act out this opposition in the same ways. Indeed, the early years of apartheid offered

xvii

multiple channels through which South Africans could move against the state – as activists, intellectuals, workers and critics. The diffuse character of this resistance cuts against the ANC's assertion of its historical primacy. And it cuts a new path through the country's past, a chaotic and less settled vision of South Africa then and now.

Unsettling the history we know, of course, comes at a cost. If we refuse to see the past as a straight and simple march to the present, if we allow ourselves to fully inhabit its darkest corners, it no longer tells such a coherent, triumphant tale. Nat's life, in many ways, has no proper narrative arc. He was making a slow slog through his life, slinging together sentences and fleeing police and sneaking kisses with white girls from the suburbs, and then, quite suddenly, he was not. That isn't the story of a martyr. Nat didn't suffer the most of any South African who went into exile, he wasn't a tortured literary genius, he never went to jail for his beliefs or watched his family be killed. His life can't be made into a symbol of the great path of human destruction apartheid cut through black South Africa. But perhaps that is what makes his story all the more worth telling. It stands for nothing but itself.

It is an often-repeated adage that journalists write the first draft of history. In fact, it would be more accurate to say that they are the gatekeepers between events and history, a kind of advance guard for popular memory. Journalists take facts at their most raw and whittle them into stories that shape the way we think about the swirl of information that surrounds us. Yet, often the writers who produce this news find themselves reduced in the sweep of history to little more than a formless byline. And in a certain sense, it is not difficult to see why. After all, where can you find someone like Nat more easily than in the pages of the magazines he wrote for? His name anchors stories of political violence, township witch doctors and the life of Winnie Mandela; of forced labour, cigar makers and the death of an infamous boxer. The writer behind these tales is not always invisible, but he is rarely the focus of the stories he tells.

History too has cast a sidelong glance at Nat. While he is not absent from it, he hovers at the edge of the frame in histories of apartheid-era journalism, literature and intellectual culture. Books, articles and films speak obliquely of a writer who moved quietly through the liberal intellectual community in 1950s South Africa, without the flashy, bitterly cynical personality that defined so many black writers of his generation. He appears observant and vaguely clever, often little more than a quotable sound-bite in some larger historical narrative. And nearly always, these small mentions of Nat come to rest on the tragic fact of his death. Distilled to these basic elements, Nat's story has passed from story to story, rarely accumulating additional detail or analysis.[7]

This book, of course, recognises the great importance of writing in Nat's life – indeed, it relies heavily on the words he wrote about himself and others. But it also tells the story of someone who was more than simply an accumulation of bylines. His story is not a news article, neat and well-bounded, cleanly ordered and easily summarised. It is a life, hefty and uneven and sprawled, treading its own path through the dense thickets of history all around it.

One

TO GET FROM THE SUBURBS north of Durban to the house where Nat Nakasa was born, now as in his time, you must cross a tightly partitioned city. The route sweeps westward, away from the ocean, through manicured, security-patrolled suburbs – an unbroken line of concrete walls boxing off the houses and swimming pools of the upper class, where the quiet is broken only by the buzz of electric fences and dogs barking at passersby. This neighbourhood eventually rambles into an industrial district, and beyond that the city gives way to township – clusters of small, brightly painted houses and shacks leaning up against the steep hills that flank the city.

I am travelling to Nat's old house with his sister, Gladys, and her stepdaughter, Jabu, who have brought me here to meet Nat and Gladys's stepmother, Mabel. Seventy years after Nat and Gladys's parents moved to Chesterville in the 1930s, she owns the house where they grew up, and Gladys wants me to see it. We brake for a chicken bobbing slowly across the road as a rusted white van barrels toward us on the wrong side of the street, its tinny speakers blasting house music in Zulu. As Jabu drives, Gladys calls out directions – left at the roadside stall painted with the vibrant red logo of a local cellphone company, then right at an elementary school, again at a vivid blue house – until the car pulls to a stop in front of a stout brick house with a pawpaw tree in the yard. A dog is pawing at the trunk as we step out, that kind of dog that seems to exist everywhere in the world – wiry and brown, with sharp-tipped ears – and greet the knot of Nakasas who have come out to meet us.

'*Sawubona,*' they say to me, laughing as my tongue trips over the response. '*Yebo, sawubona.*' Inside, in a small living room they motion for us to sit, and for several minutes I sit mutely as Zulu pings back and forth all around me – pleasantries and family gossip flying by in a language I can't understand. At some point, noticing my silence, someone hands me a thick wedge of a photo album. It is filled with mundane and private family moments. There are birthday parties and teenage girls striking silly poses against brick walls, babies and weddings, and unidentified black-and-white photos of city streets and young men leaning against vintage cars.

Then, tucked between two pages in the album, I come across a stern, posed portrait of Nat and Gladys's father, Chamberlain. He looks to be about 50 and he is writing, his face bent into an expression of deep concentration. I flip over the photo. On the back, in red marker in all capital letters, is the following inscription: 'The father of the house who was a journalist and please don't take him otherwise because his dreams had come true. He died of a heart attack because his children were in overseas so he stressed if his children are still

A Native of Nowhere

alive or not died in 1977 January 15 we'll always love u.' The words tumble out in one nearly unpunctuated stream, a curt but strangely poignant eulogy.

Reading that photo caption I am struck, not for the first time, by the vicious downward spiral that apartheid visited on Nat's family. When this photo of Chamberlain was taken sometime in the 1940s, he was a successful writer and religious pundit with a regular column in Durban's elite black newspaper, *Ilanga lase Natal*. He had five children and a house that, while small, was his own. And he was in the process of grooming his children for missionary education and a white-collar future. Stern and moralising, he lectured them to study hard and stay away from township hooligans. 'He wanted a youth that could work for themselves, rather than just running around,' Gladys told me. 'He wanted them to wake up and do something.'[1]

Not long after, however, his wife was permanently institutionalised for an unknown mental illness, leaving him alone to raise his four sons and daughter. And some years after that, two of those boys – Nat and the youngest, Moses – left the country to continue their education, but within a year of leaving, Nat was dead and Moses had disappeared, never to be heard from again. Meanwhile, in South Africa itself, apartheid battered the black middle class of which the Nakasas had been part, starving off their economic opportunities and carefully guarding the boundaries of their movements. The Nakasa siblings, ambitious and educated, still had to be out of the city by dark and were technically citizens of a separate 'homeland' that had been set up by the apartheid government for their ethnic group.

Today Gladys, the only living member of that Nakasa nuclear family, is a retired domestic worker living in a two-room government-provided house on the fringes of the township of Umlazi – twelve miles further from the city than the home where she grew up. Seventy years old, she is heavyset and must limp thirty minutes with her cane to catch the nearest bus to reach the city centre, where, when I meet her, her husband is dying in a private hospital. 'I am tired,' she tells me again and again, over dinner and in my car and through staticky phone connections, 'I am so tired.'

She speaks to me about Nat willingly but listlessly. Yes, she says, she remembers him as a child, serious and careful. He helped care for his siblings and tried to impress their father with his writing prowess. And she remembers how proud of him the family were when he went off to Johannesburg, how crushed they were when they heard of his death. But what she really wants me to pay attention to are the fissures running down the wall of her house, the unfinished rafters above us. When it rains, she tells me, the house leaks, spilling water onto their bed, their kitchen counter. No one is coming to fix it – the family waited nearly a decade on an applicant list to get this house in the first place. Retired and living on a government pension of R1,000 (about $100) each month, Gladys can usually afford to buy food for the month, a few bus rides and a bit of airtime for her cell phone. But the money frequently runs out long before the month does. When I ask her if she has kept any photographs of Nat, she stares at me silently. 'We moved so many times,' she says wearily. 'I don't know what became of them.' He is gone, her irritation with me seems to say, and whatever we remember of him, he is never coming back to help us.

On 12 May 1937, London erupted in celebration. That morning, King George VI and his wife Elizabeth were crowned in a lavish ceremony that the *New York Times* declared was 'the most expensive one-day show in the history of modern society'.[2] From Manchester to Hong Kong, in the metropole and its farthest-flung possessions, streets jammed with cheering crowds, celebrating the newest figureheads of the British Empire. That same day, at the outer reach of the empire, in a township outside Durban, South Africa, Nathaniel Ndazana Nakasa was born.

That Nat's life began at a moment of global importance seems in retrospect almost prophetic, for his youth was shaped in large part by the tremendous historical moments that intersected it. Born on the cusp of World War II, he was 11 years old in 1948 when South Africa's National Party (NP) came to power on the platform of apartheid – literally 'separateness' in Afrikaans – an event that profoundly transformed the direction of the next fifty years of the country's history, and his life with it.

However, just as one would never view Nat's legacy solely through the lens of his death, to see South Africa at the moment of his birth as a country careering uncontrollably toward apartheid misses the deep political and social contingency of that era.[3] Even the early years of National Party rule offered little reason to believe that this new entity known as apartheid would last beyond the next election – or that its ideology of rigid racial separation would cohere into a tangible political programme at all. For several years apartheid staggered forward with no fully realised destination, defining itself one election, one piece of legislation, one fiery personality at a time. Just as the young Nat's life pitched and swerved in relation to its own particular turmoil and opportunities, the country around him grew into the era of apartheid only by narrowly dodging its own potential futures.

Nat came of age in this world, his own future as undefined as that of South Africa itself. Born into the rare privilege of the black middle class, he grew up in the coastal city of Durban among the small minority of Africans in his generation with horizons that could reasonably extend beyond menial labour. But he was also the son of a mother who spent most of his childhood locked away in a mental asylum, a bright student who lacked the financial means to finish his education and, later, a black journalist without the editorial freedom to confront his country's institutionalised racism.

In a wider sense, he was also part of the last generation of South Africans for fifty years to know its country before apartheid, a place that, while rife with inequality, allowed a degree of openness and multiracialism that would never again be witnessed over the following half-century. That South Africa slowly faded away just as he came of age, and it was within this shifting of registers that his own perspectives on race took shape. His complex views on the subject as an adult – the receptiveness to stepping across racial lines, the anger at the profound unfairness of being born black – grew directly from this childhood reality. As a young man then, he stood astride two South Africas, bracing himself as the ground began to shift beneath him.

Nat and Gladys's parents, Alvina and Chamberlain Nakasa, were newly-weds when they moved to Durban in the 1930s, joining an influx of upwardly mobile Africans pouring into South Africa's metropolitan areas in the pre-war years. Hugging the Indian Ocean on South Africa's east coast, their new city was both a gritty trade hub and a pleasant – if not particularly exotic – beach town. The city centre was flanked by hills, which rolled inland toward the lush coastal province of Natal (now KwaZulu-Natal).

The sleepy port city was in many ways a curious microcosm of the British colonial project. Settled first in the mid-nineteenth century by British traders from the western Cape Colony, the town quickly grew into a hub for the emerging sugar industry in the region. But to the great chagrin of its settlers, the African people already living in the region – commonly lumped together as 'Zulus' – had little interest in working their new plantations. So they turned to another far-flung corner of the growing British Empire, India, for a new source of cheap labour. Arriving by boat on 25-year contracts as indentured servants, Indians fanned out across the new province of Natal, and when their contracts were up, many moved to the city of Durban. By the early years of the twentieth century, the city's population was nearly 30 per cent South Asian.

By the time the Nakasas arrived, many of the local Africans who once refused to work the Natal plantations had followed as well, pushed and pulled by rural poverty and the economic lure of Durban, crammed as it was with jobs in the shipyards, factories and gleaming homes of the white population, waiting to be cleaned and gardened. And though the municipal government built barrack-like 'workers' hostels' for the single men and 'native locations' for families, the pace of migration quickly strained the city's resources, forcing new arrivals to improvise, setting up shanty towns and cramming into Indian and coloured neighbourhoods.

As for the Nakasas, they moved to the fringes of the district west of the city quaintly known as Cato Manor. A series of rolling hillsides cluttered with wooden shacks, makeshift businesses, European-style houses and small farms, the neighbourhood seemed to awkwardly straddle urban and rural. But Cato Manor's scattered layout followed a certain historical logic. Once a vast farm on the fringes of Durban owned by a British colonial official (and later first mayor of the city) named George Christopher Cato, the land that became Cato Manor was gradually sold off in the second half of the nineteenth century, primarily to formerly indentured Indians who bought small plots to farm. By the early years of the twentieth century, Africans too had developed a vested interest in the neighbourhood. In addition to being one of the few places in the city where they were legally allowed to reside, it also had the advantage of open space for new migrants, far from the prying eyes of city police. Meanwhile, a large population of Indian South Africans, forced out of the city centre by increasingly racialised housing laws, joined the Indian community already living in the area, built houses and began renting plots to middle-class Africans.[4]

The Nakasas were one such family of tenants, renters of the boxy, one-storey brick house with a flat metal roof at 572 Road II, Chesterville, a nearby suburb.[5] The house may have been a simple one, but the very fact that the family could afford it at all attests to their social status. In Durban, as with other South African cities, most Africans lived in the houses where they worked as domestic employees, crowded hostels set up for day labourers, or sprawling slums at the city's edges. Municipal authorities calculated in 1947 that nearly 60 per cent of the African population in Durban were illegal squatters.[6]

What was more, most of the city's African population, legal or otherwise, worked as unskilled labourers, jobs that paid pitifully and rarely left funds for incidental extras like paying for a place to live. In 1956, domestic labourers in Durban – the most popular occupation for Africans – received an average of £72 per year, approximately 13 per cent of the median wage for whites in the city.[7] As a geographical survey conducted in the city a few years later condescendingly explained, 'a few Natives who have achieved a modest financial competence have settled down to a Western style of living, but the majority retain contact with the country and are culturally poised in a limbo between discredited tribalism and unattainable Westernism'.[8] For many of these low-paid service workers, jobs in a city remained simply the means to a different end altogether, a more comfortable life for the families they had left behind in their rural home.

Nat's parents, however, came from the tiny moderately educated African middle class and arrived in Durban with a different set of hopes and objectives. Both had attended rural missionary schools, the dominant educational institutions open to Africans of their generation, which offered a rigorous Christian education to the few who could afford it. Nearly 3,000 such schools dotted the 'native' areas of the country in the 1920s, when the Nakasas were students, educating some 216,000 pupils each year. By contrast, the state ran only 68 schools for Africans and had just 7,700 students. Even combined, however, mission and government schools educated only a small proportion of the country's five million Africans.[9] Nat's parents, then, occupied a tiny, privileged niche in black society.

Born of a lifetime of upward mobility, *izifundiswa*, or 'educated ones', as they were known, lived with a particular sense of possibility unknown to other urban migrants. Unlike the city's dockworkers and domestics, they held jobs for which they had been hired on the basis of their own skills and intellect. When the young Nakasa couple settled in Durban in the early 1930s, Alvina found work as a teacher, one of the few skilled professions open to African women in the mid-twentieth century, and Chamberlain became a typesetter and freelance writer.[10] And at night, Durban offered an array of leisure activities for moneyed Africans like them, from the mixed-race cinemas on Victoria Street to the legendary downtown tearooms – Chili's, Luthuli's, the Ngoma Club

– where black professionals huddled over cups of tea to gossip and talk politics. There were dances and concerts at the acclaimed Bantu Social Centre, night school classes and symphony performances.[11] For middle-class Africans in the city in those years, segregation remained a cumbersome reality, but not one that could completely derail the sense of possibility that the city presented.

Still, their lives were full of reminders of the boundaries that South African law was quietly building around their lives. As a young man, for instance, Chamberlain wrote frequently for the weekly *Indian Views*, a job that brought him into close professional contact with the city's Indian community and earned him the friendship of several prominent Indian journalists, including a young writer named Ismail Meer. Working side by side in the paper's office, the men were simply colleagues. But once Chamberlain and Ismail stepped out into the city, the difference in their skin colour took on a sudden heft. Ismail remembered inviting his friend to see a movie, only to see him shunted off to a different section of the theatre. 'Special seating for Natives,' the attendant barked, 'manager's order.'[12] These small indignities were part and parcel of black middle-class life as the Nakasas settled into the city and began their own family.

Soon after the couple arrived in Durban, Alvina stopped working to give birth to their first son, Kenneth, who was followed in quick succession by Nathaniel, Joseph, Gladys and Moses. By the mid-1940s, the Chesterville house was filled with the clamour of young Nakasas. For the family itself, their small measure of prosperity was knotted to their belief in the value of individual uplift and political moderation as paths to racial equality in South Africa. Steeped in the ideas of self-help and economic autonomy advocated by the black American reformer Booker T. Washington and others across the African diaspora at the turn of the twentieth century, these values percolated into the consciousness of many elites across the African continent in the decades that followed. And they found particularly fertile ground in South Africa's complex racial politics. There, they appealed to both whites – who saw them as a way to modulate African advancement – and blacks, for whom they conjured up a sense of industriousness and racial pride. Indeed, by the 1930s Washington's ideas had become part of the rhetoric of liberals of every colour in South Africa.[13]

Chamberlain himself was a tireless proponent of this creed. As a columnist for Durban's Zulu-language weekly, *Ilanga lase Natal*, in the 1940s and 1950s, he regularly churned out op-eds with moralising titles like 'There is Nothing Beyond the Culture of Respect', 'On the Decline in Respect for Pastors', and 'We Must Help Each Other at All Times'. Heavy on Bible verses and parables, these columns were peppered with advice for how to lead a better, more respectable life.

In one striking piece, he described a friendship between two teenage girls, the lovely Gugu, who dutifully cares for her home and family, and the urbane, beguiling Bajabulile, constantly needling her friend to go out to meet boys and see movies and concerts. For Chamberlain, Bajabulile represented everything wrong with city life: its materialism, its individualism, its casual hedonism. 'Today you are going to the white men's land,' he wrote, referring to the cities. 'The language that is spoken there is money-money-money. You eat through money, friendships and relationships are made by money ... Even your relatives won't visit you if they realize that you don't have money.'[14] To give in to Bajabulile, he wrote, was to give in to a life unmoored from tradition, buffeted by the constant temptations of urban existence.

The story trod a narrative path well known to Chamberlain's class: the cautionary tale of the pure rural African corrupted by city life. Fascination with the moral chasm between rural and urban Africans became the subject of many works of literature by both blacks and whites in the mid-twentieth century. These so-called 'Jim goes to Jo'burg' stories became the global face of South African literature when, in 1948, the Natal writer Alan Paton published the novel *Cry, the Beloved Country*, which told the story of a rural African priest who goes to Johannesburg in search of his wayward son, who he eventually discovers is wanted for murder. 'They go to Johannesburg,' the novel's narrator laments of his son's generation, 'and there they are lost and no one hears of them at all.'[15]

Chamberlain was obsessed by this lost generation, the newly urbanised Africans who straddled two worlds and often seemed unable to find their feet in either. In 1941, he published a slim bilingual volume on the subject, appropriately titled *Ivangeli Lokuz' Akha*, or *The Gospel of Self Help*. His short treatise promised to provide an inside view of the state of the African race, 'a race at its infant stage of growth,' he explained.[16] Sketching the turbulent history of the 'Bantu people', Chamberlain explained that his race had been dealt a difficult hand by European colonisation. Prostitution, murder, drunkenness and poverty, he wrote, had all come to South Africa courtesy of the white man. But Europeans had also lifted Africans out of darkness and ignorance, and solving present social ills could not be accomplished by retreating into African society. In fact, Chamberlain stressed that the development of the African would depend heavily on the support and camaraderie of white allies and aid organisations, whose generosity and knowledge could help Africans rise briskly through the ranks of 'civilisation'.

At the same time, he was stern in his prescription for Africans: if they wanted a way out of the cycles of poverty and dislocation, they would have to change things on their own. His treatment was both philosophical and pragmatic. If Africans aspired to be seen as civilised, he wrote, they might start by understanding that they already were so. 'The gold mines, roads and magnificent buildings which the white man regards as modern European achievements, have been constructed through the joint labour of white and black,' he explained. 'So, how can you call it a whiteman's civilization?'[17]

But even beyond recognising themselves within the 'civilised world', well-heeled Africans had a responsibility to provide for their own to lift the race from destitution. The problems caused by massive black migration to the cities, for instance, could be solved if only wealthy Africans would create a 'Bantu National Fund' to stimulate agriculture and rural enterprise and keep poor Africans from seeking work in the vice-ridden urban areas.[18] Chamberlain explained that such exercises in self-help, along with the benevolence of sympathetic whites, were ultimately the only things that could stop Africans from backsliding into a moral vacuum as they collided with the white world.

Chamberlain's worldview hung over Nat's childhood in Chesterville. Gladys remembered that her father insisted they do well in school and taught their children English from a young age, so that they could move more easily through all corridors of South African society. As parents, Chamberlain and Alvina made clear that their talk of hard work and racial pluralism was not simply rhetoric. The next generation of Nakasas should be intent on making something of themselves.

Nat lived up to these lofty expectations. The second of the five Nakasa children, he was a precocious, round-faced boy known among neighbourhood children as 'the tiny one'.[19] His sister remembered him as a serious, quiet child who from a young age always had his face hidden behind a book. 'He told me I must love school,' she said. 'I must love it and I must always work hard.'[20] That may have been a strange and serious statement for a young child, but the Nakasas were a serious bunch, forced by a sudden tragedy to grow up far quicker than they otherwise would have.

In 1944, soon after the birth of Nat's youngest brother, Moses, Alvina slid into a deep depression. Although the roots of her condition are murky – in his later years, Nat would refer to it only as his mother's 'illness' – the timing of its onset makes it reasonable to suggest that perhaps she suffered post-partum depression and never recovered.[21] Whatever the cause, mental illness presented a dark world for black South Africans like Alvina and her family, not only because of the new cracks it forced into their already strained lives, but also for the bleak choice it forced. Should the Nakasas keep their wife and mother – a hollowed-out woman who could no longer care for her children – at home with them, where at least they would have her close by? Or should they send her into the unknowable terrain of a black South African mental hospital, decrepit institutions that even a 1930s government official confessed were 'dangerous to the mental and often to the physical welfare of their patients'?[22]

While the family wrestled with the decision, Nat and his older brother, Kenneth, became de facto heads of their clan of siblings, and a lanky seven-year-old Nat with baby Moses on his hip was soon a common sight in their part of Cato Manor. Meanwhile, Alvina's mental health continued to unravel, rending gaping holes in her memory. Increasingly desperate, the family brought Alvina to William Duma, a local Baptist minister renowned for his healing abilities. There, at Wednesday prayer meetings at the Umgeni Road Baptist Church, crowded with the diseased and injured, the family asked Duma to heal Alvina. But even the man whom Chamberlain himself had praised as a 'miracle maker' couldn't undo his wife's growing madness.

Moses was only two when the family finally decided to have Alvina committed to Sterkfontein Mental Hospital near Johannesburg. The hospital, like others of its era, was characterised more by its ability to keep 'troublesome insane natives' away from the general public than by its curative qualities. Indeed, for Nat's mother and other urban Africans, white psychiatrists theorised that contact with 'civilising influences' in European-controlled cities was what broke their fragile minds in the first place, and probably would not have wanted Alvina ever to return to Cato Manor.[23] The Nakasas, too, likely knew that their mother wasn't coming back. '[When we visited her,] she didn't know who we were,' Gladys remembered. 'She was really very disturbed.'[24]

As the Nakasas wrestled with Alvina's illness, a political storm was slowly building in white South Africa. Riding on the wave of discontent about South African participation in World War II, the Rev. Dr D.F. Malan and his Afrikaner-rooted Herenigde Nasionale Party – the Reunited National Party – campaigned in the 1948 elections on a simple declaration. 'A course of equality between white and black races', Malan told his supporters, 'must eventually mean national suicide for the white race.'[25] Instead, he promised, the party would institute a system of total segregation, or, in Afrikaans, *apartheid*.

As black families like the Nakasas continued to migrate to South Africa's cities, seeking jobs that had once been the exclusive preserve of poor whites – most of them Afrikaners – the incisive simplicity of that slogan began to build momentum. 'Integration of the Natives into the economic and political life of the country' would end in the 'wrecking of white civilization', Malan promised.[26] And all around the country, people listened.

Still, on 26 May, the old guard of South African politics, the United Party (UP), and their leader, the military hero

Jan Smuts, went confidently into the national elections. With their coalition partners, they held more than twice as many seats as the National Party, and many observers around the world had already called the election in their favour. As the British newspaper *The Observer* reported, 'the general view' on the ground in South Africa was that the UP would easily be returned to power.[27] Prime Minister Smuts and the party may have acted 'very warily indeed, perhaps too warily' in addressing the 'non-European problem', it wrote, but only a major disaster could completely reverse their significant manpower advantage.[28] But both the UP and observers had underestimated the drumbeat of fear propelling many white South Africans to the polls that day. When the returns were tallied, the National Party had cleanly ousted the UP and brought a new government to power.

But the election that would shape the course of modern South Africa was little more than a procedural glitch. The National Party won only a minority of votes, but due to a provision in the constitution that allotted greater representation to rural voters – most of them Afrikaners – they carried 79 seats to the UP's 65. And what was more, as the UP piled on superfluous votes in areas they were already sure to win, the NP won several crucial contests by infinitesimally small margins. In fact, one historian has posited that if only 91 strategically placed voters out of more than one million had voted the opposite way, the outcome would have been a hung Parliament.[29] But it was not to be. The week after the election, Malan declared to his supporters, 'in the past we felt like strangers in our own country, but today South Africa belongs

A Native of Nowhere

to us once more. May God grant that it always remains our own.'[30] The party would not relinquish power for 46 years.

But if a white election was a world away from Cato Manor and Nat's childhood, the uneasy politics of race in South Africa were also on display far closer to home. On 13 January 1949, seven months after the National Party's election, on a stifling day in downtown Durban, the city cracked.

It was a humid evening, just before 5 p.m. From the onion-domed Juma Masjid mosque on Grey Street came the opening notes of the early evening call to prayer. Men laid out mats and folded their bodies towards Mecca, while nearby clusters of young Africans crowded into a municipal beer-hall for pungent sorghum beer. All around, commuters and shoppers rushed by, streaming past stands piled high with the goods of Indian traders – bolts of brilliant fabric, sculpted piles of orange and yellow spices, vats of spicy samoosas – toward the rickety buses and trains that would carry them out of the city to the townships and suburbs beyond.

From the centre of this evening rush came the first shouts – an Indian shopkeeper and an African teenage boy named George Madondo were squabbling in the street. The boy had tried to steal from him and struck one of his employees, the shopkeeper charged. Then he shoved the boy, hard. There was an ominous crack, flesh against glass, as George flew through a nearby shop window. When he stumbled to his feet, his face was bleeding.

19

On the scale of human conflict, it barely registered – a simple, everyday injustice. But that night, it stirred something, needling at the quiet sense of rage many Africans in the city felt towards their Indian counterparts. This man, perhaps, stood in for the Indian shopkeeper in their own neighbourhood, who allowed Africans less on credit than Indians, who charged prices far higher than what they could afford and never employed their sons, brothers, husbands. Or perhaps he represented their landlord, extorting ludicrous prices for shacks and old houses that were barely maintained. Whatever their thoughts on that burning summer night, it began with the simple indignity of the situation at hand: another African teenager accused of theft, belittled by an Indian shopkeeper, and left bleeding in the streets.

So someone threw a punch, or perhaps lobbed a rock. The first attack wasn't recorded. But just like that, a riot began. Along Victoria Street, along Grey Street, spilling west towards Warwick Avenue, the fighting spread spontaneously.[31] Bottles rained down from first-floor apartments and people began to smash car windows. Crouched, terrified, on their roofs and balconies, Indian families lobbed bricks and stones at the street, while Africans smashed the shop windows below. At the end of the evening, the police broke up the fighting, but they counted 62 people injured, 11 of them with fractured skulls.[32]

In the tense calm that night, news of the riot travelled across the city. Among many Africans, several mangled versions of the story circulated. An Indian man had killed a young African boy, cut off his head, and put it on display in his mosque, some said. In another version, several Africans had been killed by

Indian mobs in town. The stories were all of humiliation and violence at the hands of Indians. Through the night, groups gathered around the city to organise a response.

The next morning, a large group of African men set out for the city centre. Some carried spears, many were chanting. Around noon, they reached the city centre and fanned out into the Indian areas. The attack was quick and organised. The mob began kicking in windows and setting fire to buildings. Some attacked Indians they ran across with clubs. One policeman later recalled overhearing one man promise that this would be the end of Indians in Durban. 'You prepare the ships,' he said. 'We will see to it that they embark.'[33]

But Indian residents soon regrouped. That afternoon, in the Nakasas' neighbourhood in Chesterville, Gladys remembered looking out across the hillside to see fires spreading across the Indian areas of Cato Manor, charring the green hillside an ashy black. From there, the family could see the fighting spreading across the neighbourhood. Other witnesses in the area described the pop of gunshots, the screams of people fleeing their burning homes. Late in the afternoon, a line of twelve municipal buses arrived in the neighbourhood, carrying masses of both rioters and workers evacuated by police from the city centre. As they disembarked, a gathered crowd called out for any Indians aboard to come forward and make themselves known, or be killed.[34] It was just the kind of situation Chamberlain most feared – enraged, unemployed men with little regard for authority, suddenly given an easy situation to release their untapped rage. A perfect storm.

It's impossible to know just what the Nakasas saw that

night, but the ferocity and span of the riot made it certain they were never far from the fighting. And as the night wore on and the police drove rioters from the inner city, Cato Manor became the centre of the conflict. Leaders from the Natal Indian Congress and the African National Congress (ANC) rode through the neighbourhood streets in vans, imploring the crowds over loudspeakers to break up and go home.[35] Meanwhile, thousands of families – first Indians, then Africans – grabbed bundles of their belongings and fled. The Cato Manor police station soon overflowed with terrified residents seeking safety, even as the police fashioned a temporary mortuary on its veranda to lay out the bludgeoned and bullet-ridden bodies of the riot victims for identification.

By the next morning, a massive reserve of police from around the country had arrived in Durban to quell the fighting. As they fought with the last remaining rioters, a 'sultry and brooding quiet' descended over the city, one paper reported. Across the city, a misty fog hung overhead as the numb search for survivors and bodies in the charred ruins began. 'Pitiable scenes of misery,' one reporter wrote, describing watching panicked families comb through the rubble. A few more fights broke out, even as the leaders of the major Indian and African civic organisations in the city issued a frantic plea for residents to stay home and away from any fighting. But the worst was over.

Slowly, the cold business of tallying the horror began. Some 150 people died during the riots, and more than a thousand were injured, of whom 58 would later die from their injuries. And the toll on the fragile infrastructure of the city's working-class neighbourhoods was just as staggering: nearly 250 houses and 58 stores were destroyed, and another 1,285 houses and 652 stores badly damaged. Several rapes were reported.

In the breathless reporting on the riots, reporters had drawn repeated attention to the 'tribal' violence that had swept the city. The *Cape Times* reported 'murder and pillage' from 'chanting natives', and as the *Los Angeles Times* described the scene, the streets of Durban were filled with 'Zulu mobs ... chanting their ancient battle cries' as they roved about the city in 'an orgy of killing, arson, and looting'.[36] 'Native Mobs Beat Women and Children,' blared the headline in the local white paper, the *Natal Mercury*.[37] And when an official report into the causes of the riot was published a few months later, it bore the hallmark of the same kind of racism, explaining that Africans in cities were all but predestined to turn to violence. 'The Zulu is by tradition a warrior,' the report explained. 'The veneer of civilization which has come to him during his urban existence is but a thin covering ... this breaks under the stress of emotion.'[38]

Indeed, it was Indian homes and businesses that bore the brunt of the damage in the attacks, leaving thousands homeless and without their livelihood. But the casualty figures told a far more complex story. Among the 147 who died during the riots themselves, just 50 were Indians, while 87 were Africans.[39] The official report into the disaster would show that half the Africans killed were shot, many with guns of types not used by the police, and 18 had been stabbed to death. The rage, it seemed, had flowed from all sides, and those involved could not be easily divided into victims and perpetrators.

Instead, as the city reeled from the disaster, many began to acknowledge that the riots had been motivated by complex layers of anger on both sides. As one lawyer for both the African National Congress and the South African Indian Congress put it, the riots 'were caused not so much by antagonism between the two groups as by the conditions of poverty and oppression common to both'.[40] The bruised United Party was quick to jump on this bandwagon as well, asserting that South Africa was 'tasting her first fruits' of the 'racially repressive policies' of the National Party government.[41] For all of these observers, the riot had revealed a dark underbelly in South Africa's racial politics, a distant tremor that seemed to be constantly just beneath the surface of everyday life, awaiting the provocation that would cause it to erupt.

Still, in the aftermath of the riots, life lurched forward for both Africans and Indians in the city. Chamberlain continued to work for *Indian Views* and, sensing his second son was developing an interest in words, began to take him to the office to help set the type for the paper every Saturday.[42] Hunched over the drawers of tiny, raised metal letters, the older Nakasa taught his son how to put together a newspaper, one meticulously constructed word at a time. It is impossible to know what the two generations of Nakasas talked about on those long afternoons, or if they simply worked in comfortable silence, but the love of stacking words together, of building a good sentence and assembling clean and careful writing, carried far into the younger Nakasa's own life.

In 1951, Nat left home to attend Eshowe High School, a Lutheran boarding school in the heart of rural Zululand. As with his parents, mission education was the logical progression of his childhood, the next step toward assuming a place within the country's tiny African elite. White-run missionary education, Chamberlain wrote, provided the ethical and educational foundations for a civilised existence, teaching young people 'the gospel of Christianity and refined habits of life'.[43] That hallowed tradition was his past, and he aspired for it to be his children's future. But for the younger Nakasas' generation, the South African government had something else in mind.

Two years after Nat arrived at Eshowe, in 1953, the government passed the Bantu Education Act, codifying apartheid in the realm of education and dictating a series of crippling regulations for black mission schools. The Act built a rigid wall between the education of 'Bantus', or Africans, and that of whites. Under the terms of the new law, different races were to be educated to live in accordance with the opportunities South African society afforded them. 'There is no place for [the Bantu] in the European community above the level of certain forms of labour,' explained the Minister of Native Affairs and future South African Prime Minister, Hendrik Verwoerd. 'What is the use of teaching the Bantu child mathematics when it cannot use it in practice?'[44] For the first time, the law brought mission education directly under government control, and in order to continue receiving state funding for teacher salaries, parochial schools had to adhere to the government curriculum, a set of lesson plans explicitly designed to prepare Africans for a future in menial labour. In response, the majority of mission schools shut their doors, paving the way for the establishment of a dangerously low-quality system of public education.

Eshowe was an exception, accepting the standards of Bantu education as the price it must pay for continuing to educate black South Africans. And by all accounts, Nat thrived there. With two friends who would also go on to have careers in journalism, Obed Kunene and Lewis Nkosi, he formed the school's first student news magazine.[45] In 1954, he completed his Junior Certificate (at the end of Grade 10), something only 2 per cent of Africans at the time managed, and left school.[46] With that education, however, came a heavy paradox – no matter how many classic novels an African read or how many advanced maths problems he could complete, no matter how often his teachers had espoused religious teachings on the common humanity of the races, in 1950s South Africa he simply could not escape the colour of his skin or the alarming restrictions it engendered.

Nat, now 17, carried that weight as he returned to Durban to find work. Indeed, the city he returned to was one where Africans made up less than a third of the population, but represented more than 80 per cent of service and domestic workers.[47] The vast majority of Africans worked in the low-paying service and manual labour sectors. Indeed, the percentage of the African population working in the professions and commerce, such as medicine, teaching and business, was so small as not even to be counted in census figures.[48] Shoved headlong into this reality, Nat made a predictable choice for a man of his race and generation: he presented himself at a recruiting depot for a mining company – hoping to be sent to work on one of the gold or diamond mines in the country's interior. The job, while dangerous and back-breaking, at least promised a steady wage.

Though he later remembered the day he visited the recruiter offhandedly, at the moment the reality must have been devastating. Whereas only a generation earlier, Chamberlain Nakasa had preached the gospel of educational uplift as a way out of menial labour and poverty, his teenage son now stood at the brink of that very fate. But the gruff mine recruiter gave him a brisk look and shook his head. 'Piccanin,' he grumbled, using a slang term for a small black boy.[49] With that, the overseer sent Nat on his way, jobless, aimless and on unsure footing.

Not long after, the still unemployed Nat turned up at Durban's Bantu Affairs Department to renew his identity documents. Under the mandates of several newly minted South African laws, Africans in urban areas were required to carry at all times a detailed 'reference book', outlining where they could live and work in their city of residence.[50] Coupled with the 1950 Population Registration Act, which classified every South African into a discrete racial group, the legislation choked off the African presence in the cities, affording permanent residential rights only to those 'natives' who were either born there – like Nat – or had worked continuously for one urban employer for more than ten years. Others had to apply for rights as migratory labourers, coming and going according to white demands for labour.[51] Heaped on top of already complex restrictions on African access to the cities, these laws provided the state with a bruising means of enforcing urban apartheid.

As cornerstones of the National Party's burgeoning segregation policy, the 'pass laws' also served as a method by which, intentionally or not, the government could ensure that nearly every African who came to a city at some point broke the law. If you left work late and found yourself in a white area after hours or ran out to buy bread and forgot your reference book, the South African police could legally detain you. Between 1952 and 1962, authorities made an average of 274,000 convictions of pass law violations each year. In total, police records show approximately three million convictions over the course of the decade, committed by a population of just under three and a half million persons.[52] Although there were undoubtedly a large number of repeat offenders (and an underreporting of the African population in official census records), that still means the pass laws managed to legally ensnare a massive proportion of Africans in the cities.

For Nat, however, a pass was the price of admission for continuing to live in Durban, so he dutifully queued up at the Bantu Affairs office and waited his turn to receive the notorious document. When he reached the front of the line, the clerk – also an African – beckoned him forward to hammer out the details of the ID that both were required to carry at all times. As the two men began the process of collecting Nat's information, they struck up a conversation. Nat asked the clerk his name. Theo Zindela, he said, and before long the two had launched into an energetic discussion about tennis. By the time Nat's pass was ready, the men were making plans to meet that Saturday for a game of ping-pong.

As Theo remembered it in a slim memoir three decades later, the friendship grew quickly from there. Soon he, Nat and Nat's childhood friend, the gangly and serious Lewis Nkosi, formed 'a trio of angry young men' who met frequently to talk politics, literature and, naturally, women.[53] In those days, Theo remembered, Nat was always good for a laugh when it came to his demeanour with the ladies. A small, round-faced young man, he was earnest, smooth-talking and well dressed. Somewhere in his time in the city, he developed a habit of finding beautiful women on the street and slyly falling into step beside them, striking up a conversation that he hoped would last long enough to ask for a date. His favourite targets in this game were white women. No, he laughingly told friends, he didn't expect them to actually agree to go out with him, 'a bloody kaffir'.[54] He simply wanted to extend the offer. And anyway, he told Theo mischievously, the 'people who saw us strolling side by side, talking, didn't realise we were just quarrelling strangers. They probably thought she was my *bokkie* [girlfriend].'[55]

That was far from the only time that apartheid became the punchline in one of Nat's jokes. As Enoch Duma, another childhood friend, put it, 'We were poor. We were oppressed. We were living in fear of being terrorised by white South Africans … But we had these moments of looking at ourselves and laughing, really laughing hard, at some of the things that had happened to us.' He remembered they often mocked the cops who came to raid the backroom bars, or shebeens, operating illegally in the townships. They'd rummage through the room, find nothing, and backpedal out – all the while missing the giant drum of African beer sitting in the centre of the room covered with a swatch of cloth. These policemen had spent their entire lives surrounded by Africans – as their nannies, domestic workers, shop assistants and, now, criminal charges – and yet they still had no idea what a jug of African beer looked like. In situations like that, Duma thought, how could you help but laugh?[56]

As Nat fell into step with his friends in the city, he also secured his first job, as an entry-level labourer at a Durban engineering firm.[57] But his energies were elsewhere. In 1955, he, Theo and Lewis founded the Chesterville Cultural Club, which met weekly for play readings, jam sessions and informal debates with other young people in the area. Now comparatively well educated, Nat and his friends had cast themselves in the role of carving out a more 'respectable' culture in the poor neighbourhood where they had grown up. As Nat described it then, Chesterville was 'a paradise for vice addicts'. The township, he griped, is 'well over ten years old now [and] has no library and no entertainment centre'. The cultural club was meant to plug that gap, bringing in 'respected guest speakers' for regular talks on important topics like religion, uplift and racial harmony.[58]

Just as the cultural club began to dominate the three men's social lives, Lewis caught a lucky break in the working world.

After spending several months as a freelance writer in Durban, he received an offer to become a staff writer at *Ilanga lase Natal* ('the Natal Sun'), the city's Zulu-language newspaper. An aspiring African journalist in the city could hope for no better position. One of only seven African newspapers in the entire country in the mid-1950s, *Ilanga* had served as the cultural and political mouthpiece of Durban's black elite since the turn of the twentieth century and was well known and regarded among the city's literate Africans.[59]

Despite the paper's African audience and writers, however, it had an ambivalent relationship with the politics of black liberation. When the paper was first launched in 1903, its editor, John Dube, had proclaimed that *Ilanga* would 'keep the people informed about events and show them ways of improving themselves', a sort of gospel of self-help in journalistic form.[60] In 1935, however, buckling under the economic pressures of the Great Depression, *Ilanga* merged into Bantu Press, a national conglomerate of black newspapers owned in turn by the country's dominant white publisher, Argus Printing and Publishing. Like many other black newspapers of the era, it surfaced from this takeover in a curious state, ostensibly editorially independent, but at the same time reliant on white capital for its own survival. The resulting product had a sharp focus on social and cultural news, only gingerly broaching politics – and especially race – within its pages.[61]

A few months after Lewis began work at the paper, in early 1956, Theo landed a job there as well. Immediately, the two men turned their attention to Nat, determined to find a way for their third musketeer to join them at the newspaper.

When the man who prepared tea for the *Ilanga* office went on vacation, they jumped at their chance and had Nat hired for the position, hoping they could finagle it into something more permanent. But two weeks later, the original 'teaboy' returned from his break and Nat was once again out of a job.[62]

Lewis, however, already had his sights set on bigger things. When the Johannesburg-based *Drum* magazine, far and away the country's most widely circulated black publication, set up a satellite office in Durban, Lewis pounced on the chance to write for it. And his persistence paid off. Before the year was out, *Drum* had taken the 20-year-old onto their permanent staff and, soon thereafter, he packed his bags and moved to Johannesburg to report from the magazine's headquarters.

For Nat, Lewis's departure proved fortuitous. He quickly applied for and then received his friend's former job at *Ilanga* and signed on as a cub reporter. The paper made him responsible for a slate of short pieces – profiles, neighbourhood announcements, legal briefings and other miscellania that filled out the weekly pages – that took him around the city. However, with so few qualified Africans available for hire, a true division of labour at black papers like *Ilanga* was next to impossible. So though he was young and had never completed high school, Nat was very likely expected to report, write, photograph, edit and help proof the paper each week. Life as an African reporter, in other words, meant accepting a dizzying level of responsibility without any promise of editorial freedom in return. As a fellow black journalist, Herbert Dhlomo, wrote, 'the African journalist in most cases is under-paid, over-worked, is hampered with irritating restrictions, and is not free to speak out loud and bold.'[63]

One day in 1957, for instance, Nat was downtown working on a story when he saw a group of people gathered on a street corner. As he approached, craning his neck, he could see they were watching the police argue with a group of Africans, demanding to see their passes. As Nat drew close to the scene, he immediately reached for the camera slung around his neck. If there was about to be a dramatic arrest, he probably thought, it could make for interesting photos in the next issue.

But as he lifted the camera, one of the policemen noticed. He approached Nat and demanded to know who'd given him permission to photograph the scene. Then, without waiting for an answer, he grabbed Nat roughly and told him he was under arrest. When Nat demanded to know what for, the officer told him gruffly that the police needed to examine his camera. Suddenly both Nat and his camera found themselves in the back of a police car, on their way to the station. There, Nat demanded again and again to know the charge. Finally, a white *Ilanga* employee showed up and demanded again that the cop explain the situation.

'There's no charge,' the policeman snapped at him.

'Then why have you arrested him?'

'Because I don't want my picture appearing in those kaffir newspapers,' he spat. 'But you're working for a kaffir paper, so I guess you wouldn't know that.'

With that, he gave Nat back the camera and sent the two men on their way.[64]

The following week, the incident appeared splashed on the front page of *Ilanga* – a dramatic tale of journalism heroics complete with the stock character grumpy cop and the wide-eyed young reporter just trying to tell a story. There was anger in the tale, but there was also bravado. The young reporter – and his photos – had escaped, after all, and they were here to tell the tale.

Nat's front-page antics are a good signal that he was moving up in the journalism world, and before long he too had fixed his gaze on Johannesburg and *Drum*. The magazine, though also white-owned, had an editorial character completely unlike *Ilanga*'s – while still not overtly political, it was brazen and biting in tone and coverage. Founded in 1951, *Drum* was a young player on the black journalistic scene. It had come of age with Nat's generation, not his parents', and reflected the escalating anger of Africans living under apartheid. Such a style appealed strongly to the young writer, and he began angling for a position with the magazine.

As Sylvester Stein, then the editor-in-chief of *Drum*, remembered it, he caught wind of Nat from one of his teachers at Eshowe, who described the young writer as 'a real prodigy'.[65] With Sylvester's magazine exploding in popularity, he was looking to take on another staff writer, but finding one had proved no simple task in a country where the average educational level of an African hovered somewhere around Standard 3 (Grade 5).[66] He had already scoured the country for prospects, putting out queries to nearly everyone he knew, when he heard about Nat, and he immediately made arrangements to drive to Durban to meet him.

When Sylvester arrived in Durban, however, his job interview met a peculiarly South African obstacle – he and

Nat couldn't find a public place where they were both allowed to be. They eventually settled on a sheltered riverbank, where the editor remembered they spent an aimless afternoon fishing and swimming before finally returning to the matter at hand – Nat's future. As soon as they got to talking, Nat won Sylvester's good graces. 'He knew *Drum*, its contents and its writers, quite as well as his school books,' he wrote in his memoir.[67] That, along with his sharp intelligence and liberal political leanings, proved enough to earn Nat a job. Sylvester hired him on the spot.

Shortly before his *Drum* post in Johannesburg began in late 1957, Nat called the Durban train station to reserve a first-class berth. 'Of course, sir,' the woman on the other end told him politely. 'The ticket will be waiting for you at the station.' But when Nat arrived to collect it, the clerk balked. She was sorry, she told him, but when she'd heard his voice on the phone, she'd assumed he was white. She couldn't sell a first-class ticket to a black man.[68] Nat undoubtedly knew this, but, like tricking passersby into believing the white woman talking to him in the street was his girlfriend, reserving a first-class ticket over the phone was a clever ruse to dupe the apartheid system, and Nat relished that small power.

The law that barred the young writer from sitting in first class had existed for decades, but his trip was also marked by reminders that racial policy in South Africa was beginning to shift. When he and the other 'non-white' passengers stepped off the train at Johannesburg's Park Station, conductors directed them to a separate exit removed from the station's main concourse. The terminal had been segregated in 1949, just one year after the National Party came to power.[69] Like other institutions in South Africa, train stations had never been free of the racial hierarchy that dominated the country at large. What changed in the early years of apartheid was that the lines of racial division became more solid and impenetrable, codified into rigid laws and thus increasingly difficult to overcome through the respectability and hard work that Nat's parents' generation had championed as a surefire path to upward mobility.

In that sense, the first twenty years of Nat's life took place under the shadow of transformation, as the country catapulted headlong into the new and dark political reality that defined much of how it operated for the next half-century. The year after he moved to Johannesburg, for instance, mass removals began from his childhood neighbourhood of Cato Manor, with Africans sent to one township and Indians to another, ending its decades-long multiracial existence. But for all that changed in the course of his childhood, much also remained the same.

Apartheid did not mark a clean break from what came before it so much as a slow, uncertain radicalisation. Many of the questions surrounding black urbanisation, education and employment that festered in the halls of Parliament throughout Nat's childhood remained unanswered in his early adulthood. Just because the new government had come to power on the platform of extreme segregation did not mean they always knew what exactly that entailed, or how to go about accomplishing it. And for Nat personally, the same gripping fears and uncertainties about his future persisted before and after 1948. Apartheid or no apartheid, he was a young African man in South Africa, and that had always been a perilous perch to stand on.

Four hundred miles separated the city of Durban where Nat grew up and the metropolis of Johannesburg where he moved to work for *Drum*, but the mental space between the two was even greater. Leaving a mid-sized city on the coast, Nat found himself suddenly in the cultural and industrial heart of the country. A clever and serious young journalist, he'd already developed a strong sense of both South Africa's inequalities and the ways around them, a feature that would colour how he experienced Johannesburg and how he wrote about it. But at the moment when he arrived, before he'd set a single word down in the pages of *Drum*, he was simply a young, ambitious man intent on defining himself, slyly trying to keep one step ahead of the growing reach of state repression.

Two

ONE EVENING IN THE LATE 1950s, Nat and Lewis were walking through downtown Johannesburg when, as both later recalled, they decided to stop at a whites-only restaurant called the Texan. Inside the gaudy coffee bar, cluttered with American flags and photographs of US presidents, the young writers placed their orders with the portly American man in charge. They knew full well that he expected them to take their cups outside and drink on the pavement, but as he prepared the drinks, they exchanged a quick smile. Then Lewis pivoted on his stool and gestured to a grinning portrait of Dwight Eisenhower hanging above the bar.

'Look at that bum,' he said loudly to Nat. 'There is something seriously wrong with America's choice of heroes. Imagine the millions of American children whose ambition is to grow into the grinning emptiness which Ike symbolizes.'[1] This caught the ear of the owner and suddenly a debate was raging. As the arguments bounced back and forth, Nat and Lewis slowly drank their coffees at the bar. By the time the conversation ended, their mugs were empty and the two men paid and left. 'No one seemed to remember the colour bar,' Nat later recalled slyly.[2]

The two men had skirted the law that morning, but as soon as they stepped outside the Texan, they returned to a briskly segregated world. When the 20-year-old Nat arrived in Johannesburg in the summer of 1957, apartheid sliced across nearly all facets of life in the city, defining not only where a young African man could live and work, but also the things he could say, the people he could associate with, and even the women he could date. And each year, new legislative blows rained down from the Parliament in Cape Town, drawing the boundaries of apartheid closer and closer around Nat's life.

Nevertheless, what happened at the Texan was not an isolated event. In the early years of the young writer's time in Johannesburg, he found himself enmeshed in the city's community of mainly black artists and intellectuals, who came together in what he deftly termed 'fringe country': 'a social no-man's-land, where energetic, defiant, young people of all races live and play together as humans'.[3] Educated, uninhibited and relentlessly clever, the men and women of fringe country chose to challenge apartheid not through overt protests, but simply by refusing to let it dictate their daily social and intellectual pursuits. They formed jazz clubs and dissident newspapers, wrote musicals and published novels, attended multiracial parties and dated across the colour line, carving out a pulsing physical and mental space for black thinkers and white bohemians against the foreboding backdrop of a racially repressive state. Central to the existence of fringe country was the idea that freedom did not exist because of government legislation or political rhetoric; it didn't come from mass strikes or participation in 'the struggle'. Instead, freedom was the thing that happened when two black men sat down in a white coffee bar and convinced the proprietor to serve them – a tiny, subversive act that shifted the paradigm, if only for a moment.

This subversive culture reacted to the injustices of apartheid, but it also existed because of them. Apartheid gave fringe country, and the intellectuals who inhabited it, the sharpness, urgency and dark wit that characterised both their lives and their work. And the incoherence of the National Party's ideology and policy in its first decade in power allowed intellectuals like Nat a range of movement – albeit limited – to act out their resistance.

However, Nat moved to Johannesburg in the twilight of fringe country, at a moment when the antics of trying to get served at a white restaurant were giving way to much more grave struggles – avoiding having your work banned from publication, ducking arrest and prison time, deciding whether or not to go into exile. Not only intellectuals but also political activists faced the question of how to navigate shrinking channels of dissent. As the government tightened its grip on dissidents of all stripes, it became a constant battle for Nat and his cohort to maintain an identity more profound than the racial categorisation stamped on their identity documents. The small freedoms of the South Africa they had known as children receded further and further, leaving in their place a vicious police state and a country battered by its escalating battles with itself.

A Native of Nowhere

When Nat stepped off the train from Durban in Jo'burg's bustling Park Station in 1957, he found himself suddenly in the city he regarded as the centre of the world. In his imaginings, Johannesburg had always been a near-mythic place, 'the throbbing giant which threw up sophisticated gangsters, brave politicians, and intellectuals who challenged white authority'.[4] Here was South Africa's brave frontier town, the scrappy gold-mining camp at the fringes of a colonial empire that had grown up to be one of Africa's largest cities. And even several decades after its founding, Johannesburg retained its perpetual sense of incompleteness. The scrubby Highveld that surrounded the city was quickly being papered over by townships, with its fringes reaching further and further into the brittle plains. The feeling of newness about the city also made it a gruff kind of place. 'No doubt it was an ugly city,' Lewis wrote, filled with 'brash vulgar buildings ... skyscraper canyons and scarcely any parks or water in sight'.[5]

A decade after the National Party's accession to power on the platform of apartheid, the sprawling metropolis reeled from newly enforced patterns of segregation. Under the Group Areas Act of 1950 and its subsequent amendments, South African cities were divided into a jigsaw puzzle of 'zones' where only a single racial group could live and work. In Johannesburg, the Act spelled the end of the township of Sophiatown, the first neighbourhood where Nat lived in the city and one of its most vibrant enclaves of multiracialism.

At the moment that Nat moved to the city, the bulldozers

had already been rumbling through Sophiatown for three years, and large swathes of the neighbourhood lay razed, its inhabitants scattered to other, more distant peripheries of the city.[6] The township had drawn the government's ire because here, as in Nat's childhood neighbourhood of Cato Manor and Cape Town's District Six, racial integration was a lived reality.[7] Africans shared streets with people of Chinese, Indian, white and mixed descent, frequenting the same stores, schools and shebeens in a community drawn together by the cross-racial experience of poverty. And for those of African descent, the neighbourhood held another salient feature. Following the 1923 Urban Areas Act, which strictly delineated the areas where blacks could live, Sophiatown had been one of the only places in the Johannesburg area where Africans could legally own land.[8] So the corrugated-iron shacks of day labourers jostled up against the middle-class houses of prominent black leaders like Dr A.B. Xuma, the president of the African National Congress.

The iconic resonances of Sophiatown's multi-race and multi-class existence meant that even as the township stared down bulldozers and wrecking balls, it remained the cultural centre of gravity for many Johannesburg artists and intellectuals. As the writer Bloke Modisane, a friend of Nat's, later described it, Sophiatown 'took the ugliness of life in a slum and wove a kind of beauty', establishing cross-cultural relationships among its inhabitants that felt 'far richer and more satisfying ... than any model housing could substitute'.[9] As Lewis put it, Sophiatown was 'Harlem-like', a symbol of black 'arrogance, resilience, and scorn for the white suburb from which he was excluded'.[10] By the time Nat arrived in Johannesburg, the physical Sophiatown was in the process of being wiped from the map, but it survived as shorthand for the boundary-less urban life that African intellectuals sought to recreate elsewhere in coming years, and its untimely death as a warning of the precarious quality of this existence.

Hired by Sylvester Stein back in Durban, Nat went immediately to work for *Drum*, a popular monthly news magazine focused on African life. It had an eclectic mix of coverage, from South African politics to sports to pin-ups of popular models.[11] The young publication dated back only to 1951, when a mining heir named Jim Bailey, son of the Randlord Sir Abe Bailey, used a piece of his father's fortune to buy a failing news magazine, *The African Drum*, and set about transforming it from a projection of white views on the black community into an African-centred enterprise that appealed to township readers. 'I ma[de] sure that blacks did the writing and not whites,' said Anthony Sampson, an Oxford chum of Bailey's who became the new *Drum*'s first editor. 'It broke a long tradition of white liberals interpreting black life.'[12] That pitch was an easy sell to many black writers. The magazine soon attracted a cadre of talented young African, Indian and coloured journalists hungry to portray a world they had rarely seen in print: their own.[13]

From the outset, *Drum* was immensely popular. In 1952, an awed *Time* magazine correspondent reported that the 'teeming Negro and colored shantytowns of Johannesburg' came alive with excitement on its publication day. As delivery trucks moved through the township streets, the reporter declared, hundreds swarmed around the vehicles to buy the magazine.[14] *Drum*'s wide appeal lay in its ability to reach across class lines in the black community, peddling elegant literary journalism alongside gossipy celebrity portraits and sensationalist crime pieces. Each month's cover featured an eye-catching black model, while the inside pages revealed muckraking investigative features, including an exposé on the conditions in African prisons and an African writer's personal essay on being arrested while attempting to attend services at a white church.[15] It was 'a bit of Fleet street with a bit of black academia mixed into a newsroom', said Joe Thloloe, who wrote for the magazine's sister weekly, *Golden City Post*.[16] That distinctive mix allowed *Drum* to reach a far wider audience than any previous publication written by black South Africans, and helped catapult the magazine into the international spotlight. With 240,000 copies of each issue printed by the mid-1950s, *Drum* circulated throughout the newly and soon-to-be independent states of Africa, including Kenya, Ghana, Nigeria and Sierra Leone, and was the most widely circulated African publication in any language.[17]

For readers in and outside South Africa, *Drum* became an internal source on the frenetic universe of the township, with its grimy shebeens where young people gathered to talk late into the night, and its *tsotsis*, the flamboyant, American-inspired gangsters who roamed the narrow streets in chrome-covered cars. Here, couples walking home from all-night jazz concerts met the eyes of miners and domestic workers commuting into the city each morning, many lived day-to-day and a generation of young people took as their credo 'live fast, die young, and have a good looking corpse'.[18] The pages of *Drum* revealed a world that was fast-paced and intellectually cutting edge, but also dangerous, decrepit and desperately poor. As Lewis Nkosi once described Johannesburg, it was 'dense, rhythmic ... swaggering and wasteful, totally without an inner life'. And like the world for which it served as a mouthpiece, the magazine entangled itself deeply in the quotidian, creating an unfocused portrait where the immediate realities of poverty and racial exploitation ruled above nearly all else.

By the time Nat arrived in 1957, *Drum*'s chaotic envisioning of black urban life had brought it to the apex of its renown, and launched the careers of a cadre of dazzlingly talented black writers and photographers. As a young man with literary aspirations, Nat had no doubt read the witty short stories of the assistant editor Can Themba, a pioneer of the fictionalised literary journalism that became immensely popular in the United States over the next decade.[19] He knew of Todd Matshikiza, the legendary musician and jazz writer who was said to approach his typewriter 'as if it were a cross between a saxophone and a machine gun', and Henry Nxumalo, author of many of *Drum*'s most biting investigative pieces under the pseudonym 'Mr Drum', who was murdered while reporting on an underground township abortion ring in early 1957.[20] He had seen the photographs of Ernest Cole and Peter Magubane, whose iconic images of urban life and anti-apartheid protests circulated globally to accompany pieces about the plight of South Africa. All of these men – many of them not much older than Nat himself – stood at the summit of the South African artistic universe he wanted so powerfully to join.

And Nat's father these men were not. Educated and coming of age at the moment when segregation cohered into apartheid, this generation of writers carried themselves brashly, rejecting their literary predecessors as conservative and woefully romantic, lacking the bite to respond to the dangerous world they inhabited. The new generation, on the other hand, prided themselves on being uninhibited, indulgent and immensely gifted. They saw themselves not as an extension of either the 'mediocre' black South African literary tradition or the community of white liberal South African novelists, but rather in the mould of the Harlem Renaissance. They were figures at the crossroads of a literary and social revolution who could redefine the meaning of blackness one photograph, short story or jazz piece at a time. Much like the 'New Negro' of the United States in the 1920s, the *Drum* writers styled themselves as prototypes of a 'New African' with a strong sense of identity and racial pride.[21]

These men wrote – and lived – with a breathlessness born of both their youth and their constant struggle to outrun apartheid.[22] But the system was quickly closing in on them and their intellectual freedom. In 1950 the Union of South Africa had passed the Suppression of Communism Act, a law whose stated purpose was to ban the Communist Party of South Africa and control the dissemination of Marxist literature within the country. The law, however, defined communism in part as 'any doctrine or scheme ... which aims at bringing about any political, industrial, social, or economic change within the Union by the promotion of disturbance or disorder' or which 'encourag[es] feelings of hostility between the European and the non-European races of the Union'.[23] This sweeping definition stretched to include nearly any anti-apartheid activity, and the Act became a central legislative tool by which the state snuffed out resistant voices from the 1950s onward.

Individuals convicted under the law faced a draconian penalty known as banning. A ban prevented them from engaging in journalism, being quoted in any publication, meeting in groups of more than three, holding public office or leaving a designated area of the country.[24] It spelled the instantaneous end of a writer's career within South Africa, and thus anyone who wished to remain active in the news media trod a dangerous line between reporting the truth and avoiding suppression. As the *Drum* journalist and poet Mongane Wally Serote described it, the possibility of banning forced writers into the awkward task of 'showing the evils of apartheid without directly condemning it'.[25] Darting around the outskirts of the permissible gave rise to a biting, witty and indirect style of writing in the pages of *Drum*. The publication thrived on this cleverness, but it was an unstable way to flourish, one beset with the constant danger of what could happen if you stepped an inch too far out of line.

All of this greeted Nat as he arrived at the *Drum* headquarters for his first day of work in late 1957. For the headquarters of a multinational magazine, the publication's office was rather unassuming, a 'gaunt building' as one editor described it, at the edge of the city centre, in a rambling district filled with small factories, overgrown empty lots and a fleet of used-car dealerships. A few blocks away stood the city's 'Non-European Affairs Department'. The sinister building always had a long line of Africans snaking out of the door, nervously awaiting the pass or permits that would allow them to stay in Johannesburg. But despite this foreboding backdrop, the inside of the *Drum* offices crackled with energy, a smoky collection of glass-partitioned rooms filled with the constant patter of typewriters and jaunty conversation.[26] And little did Nat know, as his future colleagues awaited his arrival, that he had become the centre of their talk. Everyone was poised to see this 'razor-sharp journalist from Durban' whom Sylvester Stein had told them so much about.

But whatever image of sophistication Stein may have conjured up about his new recruit, it shattered the moment Nat walked through *Drum*'s doors. As Can Themba remembered vividly seven years later, 'He came, I remember, in the morning, with a suitcase and a tennis racket – ye gods, a tennis racket! We stared at him. The chaps on *Drum* at that time fancied themselves to be poised on a dramatic, implacable kind of life. Journalism was still new to most of us and we saw it in the light of ... heroics ... decidedly not in the light of tennis.' The young man, he continued, 'had a puckish, boyish face, and a name something like Nathaniel Nakasa. We soon made it Nat.'[27]

Before long, Can had invited him, just as he had Lewis before him, to stay temporarily in his flat at 111 Ray Street in Sophiatown, a place he'd nicknamed 'The House of Truth'.

A Native of Nowhere

It was a baptism by fire for the moral stalwart from Durban, who just months before had been calling meetings of a township social club meant to encourage a more 'respectable' culture among black youth. For years, Can's place had been a legendary social spot in *Drum* circles, where one could spend a long and winding night with a bottle of brandy and a heady dose of high-brow conversation – at least for as long as the party-goers could keep up. Friends and colleagues packed in for raucous parties that often lasted through the night. Can recalled one night surveying his room to find 'casualties lying all over ... on my bed, on the studio couch, sprawled across the floor'. The *Drum* photographer Peter Magubane remembered Nat's shock at encountering the place. He 'had never seen anything like it before. There was just one big room – people are playing cards here, lovers are smooching here. The truth was told there.'[28]

Penetrating that world required a certain machismo unfamiliar to Nat, who at first found himself on the edges of the magazine's social world. 'In some ways we despised Nat because he wasn't one of us,' said Joe Thloloe. He wasn't a Jo'burg boy, and worse still, he clearly wasn't much of a drinker. He took his brandy with Coke, Joe remembered, and after one drink he'd stand up, tip his hat, and say, 'Chaps, I'm off.' 'In fact he would even leave some of the drink in the bottle!'[29]

But the *Drum* staff did their best to introduce new writers to their social scene, and Can led the charge. A man of crackling, constant energy, the former high-school teacher put little stake in sobriety – or the people who practised it. By the time Nat arrived at *Drum*, he'd become the go-to figure in the office for breaking a new writer in to the *Drum* social mores. He liked to call rookie reporters over to his desk at midday and ask for a favour. When the reporter said yes, Can thrust an empty Coke bottle into his hands and pointed him in the direction of the nearest shebeen. 'Bring me a Can Themba Coke,' he'd say. 'They'll know what I mean.' And sure enough, this was an order that bar owners all around the city recognised: a splash of Coke topped with a full glass of brandy. It was Can's midday palate cleanser – and a reminder to the writer that *Drum* didn't particularly care if you were sober or not, so long as your work got done. In fact, as another writer for the magazine observed, sometimes it seemed the editors felt that 'only a drunk reporter' could 'get the big stories'.[30]

Nat may not have been a big drinker, but he quickly grew to love shebeens, the smoky speakeasies where Africans, who were legally prohibited from purchasing alcohol at any non-government-run establishment, gathered to drink, talk and be seen. Presided over by the iron fist of a matriarch known as a 'shebeen queen', these illegal drinking dens were cached in backrooms and stashed away behind downtown storefronts. They served smuggled liquor and tall bottles of Castle Lager to a wide spectrum of humanity – 'teachers, businessmen, clerks, showgirls, payroll robbers, "nice-time" girls and occasionally, even renegade priests', as Lewis Nkosi wrote. In a way, they were black South Africa's answer to the British pub: a drinking joint but also the anchor of a social universe. Blacks lived 'on the fringes of South African society', as Nat said, so it only made sense that they drank on them too.

Part of the appeal of shebeens, of course, was their illegality. Technically, blacks could only drink at glum, government-run beer-halls, but in reality the authorities were quite willing to turn a blind eye to the back-alley drinking joints scattered across the city. In time, a system had developed. When people in a neighbourhood heard the police coming, they'd whistle or yell, '*Amaphoyisa!*' (Police!) In a second, the patrons had stashed their liquor in their stomachs or beneath their seats, and when the cops burst in, they found a room full of people gathered around a record-player or huddled over a game of cards – not a drink in sight. Then again, they rarely looked too closely before ushering the shebeen queen into the next room to 'negotiate' the charges.

The geography of the *Drum* social world was built around these extra-legal drinking spots. An evening might begin at Aunt Suzie's on Eloff Street, a few blocks from the office, whose main charm was that it stood just down the road from the Marshall Square headquarters of the Johannesburg police. The brazen Aunt Suzie became so good at talking – and paying – her way out of being shut down that the raids became half the fun of visiting her place. Aunt Suzie's was where you took white friends and foreign visitors, hoping the police might make their weekly call and give your friend a show.[31] In the meantime, she filled her small lounge to capacity with drinkers and, when the place was too packed to accept even one more, escorted the overflow into her bedroom. 'We'd be sitting on her four-poster bed drinking when the cops came bursting in,' the journalist Leslie Sehume remembered.[32]

Just south of the office was Whitey's, or the White House,

on Albert Street, and a bar that Can loved (in part, no doubt, for the irony of its name) called the Church. But Nat's favourite was a little spot on Mooi Street called the Classic. From the street, it looked like a dry-cleaners. And when you went inside, sure enough, the heavy-lidded man behind the counter would gladly take an order for a pressed shirt or a bag of washing. But behind the store was a small backroom, crammed with tables and chairs and a short bar. The place was strategically placed between the offices of *Drum*, the white liberal *Rand Daily Mail*, and the left-wing *New Age*, so it drew in a large crowd of journalists. 'When we didn't have much to do, when we were bored or when we were trying to shirk duties, we'd run away to the Classic,' said the *Drum* staff writer Juby Mayet. It wasn't really a dereliction of duties, Joe Thloloe explained, 'because if a news editor wanted you he'd pick up the phone and say, I've got an assignment for you and you'd go up to the office and get it.'[33]

Nat participated in these drinking sessions as much as anyone. 'He was just light on petrol,' said Juby. 'He couldn't hold his liquor at all.' After a beer or two, he'd usually push back his glass for the night, staying on to chat as his friends grew glassy-eyed and raucous. But once in a while, Nat would keep pace with them. On one of these nights, Juby said, a crowd of *Drum* writers had gone off 'to the nearest watering hole' in Sophiatown in the magazine's old Morris Minor. At some point during the evening, Nat got up and slipped out of the bar. When Juby and others followed him, they saw him getting into the *Drum* car. The magazine's driver rushed outside just in time to see Nat pulling away from the kerb.

'Hey,' he screamed after him as the car chugged away down the dark street, 'where are you going? Get back here!' The crowd stood in the street for a minute watching the car recede, the driver still frantically yelling about how Nat was 'drunk as all' and 'going to smash it'. Then, suddenly, the little Morris Minor shuddered and stopped in the middle of the road. Juby and the others ran out to see what had happened. When they got to the car, they saw Nat passed out, his head slumped on the steering wheel.[34]

On another occasion, Nat was at a party thrown by Francie Suzman, the daughter of the anti-apartheid MP Helen Suzman, at their house in Hyde Park. Pleasantly inebriated, he had slipped away from the party to give himself a tour of the house. A few minutes later, Lewis noticed his friend missing and went out to find him. But there was no trace of him in the house. Then, peeking into the Suzman parents' room, Lewis saw something move beneath the bed. When he got closer he saw it was Nat, snoring pleasantly on the floor. When Lewis woke him up and asked him what he was doing, he smiled and mumbled pleasantly about 'wanting to see how the other half lived'.[35]

Drum's frenetic social culture points to the urgency with which its writers lived in a state that was intent on siphoning off even their most basic rights. In shebeens and offices, on the city streets and in their cramped township homes, Nat and his cohort formed deep friendships that were lived with the kind of immediacy of people who knew their world could come apart tomorrow. Any day they could be arrested for failing to carry a pass, drinking in an illegal establishment, or fraternising with white writers and artists. They could even, like *Drum* reporter Henry Nxumalo, be murdered on the streets of their beloved townships. 'People live haphazardly, in snatches of a life they can never afford to lead for long,' Nat wrote.[36] And they came together, socially, intellectually and artistically, in fringe country, the informal, multiracial association of intellectuals who chose to resist apartheid simply by attempting to live as if it did not exist. 'Some people call it "crossing the colour line",' he said. 'You may call it jumping the line or wiping it clean off. Whatever you please. Those who live on the fringe have no special labels. They see it simply as LIVING.'[37]

In fringe country, nothing was contingent on political toil or long years of participation in 'the struggle'. For writers, dissidents and intellectuals like Nat, existing beyond the colour bar was an end in and of itself, a direct social challenge to the distinct racial and social boundaries laid down by the apartheid system. And it was simply a way to get on with life, to hell with the repercussions. 'We believed', he wrote, 'that the best way to live with the colour bar in Johannesburg was to ignore it.'[38]

After he'd worn out his welcome with Can, Nat refused to move out of the city, to the neatly ordered townships yawning out into the veld where he could legally rent a house. Instead, as he described it, he preferred to live nowhere at all. In the beginning he would sleep at his desk or angle for a place to stay when friends invited him to dinner. It was either that, he told friends and colleagues with a shrug, or staying at the grim workers' hostels huddled on the edges of the city.

Once, he said, he'd called up one of the hostels just to see how they would react to him. Putting on a fake British accent, he asked if the place could accommodate his 'boy'.

'We are only taking special boys now,' the superintendent told him. 'Boys employed in the essential services: milk delivery boys, sanitation boys, and so on.'

'Jolly good,' Nat's white alter ego shot back. 'My boy is actually quite special ... he is a journalist.' He heard a hesitation on the other end.

'Well,' the man began, 'I can't promise anything.'

Nat never went to the hostel. Instead, the task of his homelessness morphed into a game. As rush hour began, he would follow the crowds spilling out from downtown office blocks. But instead of going anywhere, he crisscrossed the city centre until it emptied. Then, slipping into the offices of the *Rand Daily Mail*, where he had friends, he would read foreign newspapers late into the night. 'Friends who invited me to their flats soon got used to me showing up for a bath in addition to dinner and a drink,' he later wrote.[39]

At *Drum*, he befriended the night watchman, a 'tall, very dark man, always in blue overalls'. In the dark and empty offices, they would talk politics for hours. The watchman, Nat remembered, wanted desperately to know 'what the whites are saying now'. And when Nat travelled north to the manicured suburbs where his white friends lived, they demanded to know exactly the opposite: how it was to live as a black man in Johannesburg. Fumbling for an answer, Nat quickly realised he knew almost nothing about township life, having never lived there. 'I wanted to be in town,' he recalled later, 'not five or fifteen miles outside.'[40]

For the first eighteen months he lived in Johannesburg, he later wrote, he 'wandered without a fixed home address'.[41] One friend, Leslie Sehume, remembered he 'fell into a vagrant sort of life', staying for a while with a Jewish girlfriend and her communist parents in the white suburbs. But he rarely stuck around long enough to arouse suspicion – or even for his friends to keep tabs on where he was. 'I don't think I ever went to see Nat and Lewis where they lived,' said Francie Suzman. 'I don't even think I knew where they lived, come to think of it.'[42]

The trio met, instead, at a café in Fordsburg, the city's Indian neighbourhood, where, as some recalled, Nat later rented a single room in a dingy hotel.[43] There, they could gather at a number of restaurants that catered to cash above skin colour. There was the Crescent Restaurant, a popular student spot that ran a weekly live jazz night. And nearby stood Uncle Joe's, a local curry joint that hosted regular jam sessions and stood a stone's throw from the local police station. Even as music blasted from its open windows and clusters of white students spilled outside for a smoke, however, the cops never once raided the place. Probably, Nat quipped, because 'Uncle Joe gave them take away food on credit'.[44]

Dropping in from the nearby University of the Witwatersrand and the bohemian high-rise suburbs of Yeoville and Hillbrow, the white students whom Nat encountered in Fordsburg, much like him, were bored with their carefully partitioned space in the city. They had a 'general eagerness, often pretentious' to make black friends, he remembered, but it was better than the alternative. And for many of the students, despite living in a country where more than 80 per cent of the population was not white, those nights in Fordsburg were the first time they had ever encountered a genuinely multiracial social scene, where they interacted with blacks who were not their nannies and domestic workers, store assistants and street sweepers. 'Sometimes I was aware that I was walking from my totally white world [at Wits University] into this other world,' recalled Francie. 'It was quite shocking ... and stimulating!'[45]

But it was a precarious life, especially if you happened to fall on the wrong side of the colour bar. Each evening, a legal switch flipped in Johannesburg proper. Africans, free to move through the area during the day as long as they had work, had to be out. To stay behind was to risk arrest. White editors at *Drum* who wanted their writers to stay late at work, or just wanted to give them some leeway to move about the city, had to write them a permission slip to carry in case they were stopped by police. David Hazelhurst, a *Drum* editor in the early 1960s, said that the key was for it not to look as though your note was playing some kind of trick on the police. One should, for instance, steer clear of referring to one's black employees as 'men'. Or seeming too fond of them. 'My boy is working late for me tonight' was a good standby – just terse and uncaring enough not to catch anyone's attention.[46]

But for Nat, there was something else at stake in his attempts to skirt residential segregation: the longer he stayed out of the townships, the more distant from them he felt. 'I knew very little' then, he later confessed in a column for the *Rand Daily Mail*, about how most Africans lived. He was always 'much more at home in the suburbs than in the townships', remembered his colleague Harry Mashabela.[47] Even in his later years in the city, after he'd moved to the townships, friends said, he maintained for years an almost bizarre distance from them.

One day around 1960, for instance, Nat was walking through town when a car rolled up beside him. The driver was Thabo Mbeki, then the teenage son of one of the ANC's top brass and, later, president of South Africa, and beside him was another young activist, Duma Nokwe. Nat was then staying in Soweto, and Thabo asked if he needed a lift home. He accepted eagerly and slid into the backseat, but when Thabo asked for directions to his house, the writer couldn't tell him which way to go. The men were forced to circle through the township until they found it.

To Thabo, Nat's disorientation was symptomatic of the larger refusal of intellectuals to engage politically with the apartheid system. 'Yes there was something of a rebellion, of a refusal to be identified, to be ghettoised, to say "no" [to apartheid's restrictions],' he said. 'But then there's a small problem – you get a Nat Nakasa who doesn't even know where he lives.'[48] Where he lived, to Thabo, was not only at a township address outside Johannesburg, but also in the world that racial division had created, a world whose bounds could not be effectively slipped by simply pretending they didn't exist. The activist's deep frustration with Nat – and the wider *Drum* social culture – came from what he perceived as the magazine's total refusal to challenge the status quo. Its writers recorded a dangerous and indulgent urban black social culture built on liquor, women and crime, but they rarely seemed to judge or challenge it. For someone like Thabo, men like Nat were conflating their disdain for racial discrimination with true revolution.

For the writers and artists in Nat's circles, however, there was nothing apolitical about the way they lived, whether it was in the township or the city. 'The mere fact that you are not white politicises your life,' Juby Mayet told me. 'Your whole life is dictated by the fact that you can't travel on that tram, you can't sit in that cinema, you can't eat in that café, send your children to that school. Living like that, what else can you be but political?' Indeed, both Thabo and Nat moved in social circles that played their ideals out on the pages of their daily lives, illegally seizing what they felt convinced they had a right to: a world beyond the colour bar. 'This is how we lived,' said Ann Nicholson, a white ANC activist and one-time girlfriend of Thabo's, 'in a multiracial group to which we were all dedicated.'[49]

But the blows were coming quickly. The Immorality Act. The Suppression of Communism Act. The Bantu Education Act. The pass laws. Each new legal barrier brought new cause to flout the law, first in the private sphere and then, for activists, increasingly in the public eye as well. 'The very conditions under which [Africans] live incite us to insubordination,' Nat wrote, mirroring a sentiment often expressed by resistance leaders. 'Just being an African in itself is almost illegal.'[50]

After a year and a half of wandering without a fixed address, Nat settled finally with Lewis in Hillbrow, a hip white neighbourhood near the city centre. Packed with sleek new high-rises, the suburb was a bohemian enclave. In Hillbrow live music spilled out of cafés and bars late into the night and terraced restaurants were filled with artists and writers chain-smoking and plotting their latest projects. It was also a place that, even a decade after the National Party came to power, had a reputation for turning a blind eye to residential segregation laws. Tucked in among the young white crowds of Hillbrow were a scattering of black residents, illegally renting from landlords willing to look the other way in exchange for higher rent. Nat and Lewis were two such tenants.

'We used to go out with them there on a Friday night,' remembers Enoch Duma. 'You had all these cultures mixing together in Hillbrow – the young white people, the Indians, the blacks who were sleeping in white Johannesburg.' He remembered Nat telling him that he would much rather live in a place like this, keeping a low profile, than in one of the dusty matchbox houses in Soweto. In white areas, he said, 'you had nice clean streets, enough space, a bigger flat.'[51]

But Nat and Lewis were not content simply to live in a white area and haunt its bars. They wanted to push the boundaries even further. So, as Lewis later recalled, they decided to place an ad in a white Johannesburg newspaper. 'Wanted,' it read, 'white maid for two black journalists living in Hillbrow. Must not mind sleeping in.'[52] 'Contrary to our sardonic expectations,' Lewis wrote later, 'the newspaper in question published the ad and caused a considerable stir.'[53]

A Native of Nowhere

No one seems to remember what paper the ad was placed in, but wherever it was, it would have been in good company. 'Wanted: Housekeeper, Jewish or Gentile' read one ad in *The Star* in April 1959. Another the same month in the *Rand Daily Mail* requested a 'European housekeeper' and told the applicant to 'phone for particulars'. 'European woman ... for a private home' read another ad, and 'Wanted: European Household Help, Part Time' (*The Star*, October 1959).[54] In a country cleaved apart by race, it seemed, some people wouldn't step across the line for anything, even household help.

In every paper, requests for domestic help were nestled in among the thin columns of ads, which revealed the woefully insular world of white Johannesburg. Every day, the major white papers filled page after page with reward offers for the return of pure-bred poodles and Alsatians, announcements of golf tournament winners, and for-sale ads for rooftop penthouses. 'LOST', one ad read frantically, 'small brown dachshund bitch wearing plaid coat with red ribbons'. Across the page, in squashed, tiny print, would-be employers searched for a 'plantation manager' (perks included a 'free house servant'), an upmarket menswear salesman, or a church organist. The only clue that these papers were printed in a country that contained people who weren't white was queries for black labour, an 'intelligent African boss boy', perhaps, or a 'housegirl/nanny'.[55] Lewis and Nat's ad, wherever it was, would have stood out then not only for its galling proposition that a white woman work for a black man, but also for the fact that it was placed by a black man in the first place.

So, did the men find what they were looking for? According

to one friend, the calls began to flood in. 'Let's just say,' Enoch Duma told me with a sly smile, 'they had a whole lot more than one applicant to choose from.' But what happened next isn't clear. They ending up hiring a girl, a nice Jewish girl from the suburbs, some say. The *Drum* publisher, Jim Bailey, later insisted he had met 'the sporting lass ... [who] was good enough looking but very tall and thin'.[56] Others insisted, no, no, the whole thing was just an elaborate joke. They never intended to actually take in a white maid. As Enoch remembered it, the whole affair had ended in a confrontation with their building's owner, who summarily sent his trouble-making black tenants packing. 'By the time Lewis and Nat called off the search, the story had spread all over town,' Enoch Duma said. 'People were saying, "Who the hell do they think they are?"'[57]

Two decades later, a Johannesburg theatre company envisioned its own ending to the story in a play called *Sophiatown*. In this version, a Jewish girl named Ruth comes to live with Jakes, 'a *Drum* magazine journalist and intellectual', at his home in Sophiatown. 'I guess I just wanted to see what the other side of the world looked like,' she tells him eagerly when she moves in. Weeks later, the mass removals from the suburb begin, cleaving their delicate friendship in two. 'Look,' Jakes tells her, 'to be frank – there is plenty that you'll never understand because you'll always be looking from the outside.'

'In that case,' she shoots back, 'I'm a lot like you. You're always looking from the outside, watching.'[58]

Three

'DO BLACKS HATE WHITES?' blared the headline of *Drum*'s cover story in November 1958, Nat's first for the magazine. The story was an 'investigation into the most difficult, most critical issue in our country, in our time', its opening lines announced. In fact, the question had seemed to hover over much of the magazine's content that year, from stories of the African independence movements sweeping the continent to profiles of rioting factory workers and spot news pieces on protests against forced removals – all of them haunted by the question of apartheid and the chasms it was opening in South African society.

For his piece, Nat had collected the testimonies of a wide spectrum of black South Africans – a singer, a priest, a herdsman, a doctor, an activist – concluding that what the majority felt was 'not hate then – quite. Suspicion. Distrust. Resentment. And guilt.' Along with a piece the following month casting the opposite question – 'Do Whites Hate Blacks?' – the richly reported article was by far Nat's most significant piece from his first year of reporting at *Drum* – and his most personal. 'It is the correct, the accepted thing on the White side to show a cold hostility, if nothing worse, towards the black,' the 21-year-old wrote. 'This harsh voice is now producing a black echo. The black man who still maintains social or friendly contacts with whites is being thought of as a "sell out"!'[1]

The charge of selling out to the white establishment was one that had stalked Nat from the moment he started working at *Drum*. 'People felt like he saw a lot of things through white eyes,' David Hazelhurst, a *Drum* editor, said. 'To an extent,' said the white journalist Allister Sparks, 'I think he simply felt closer to young white folk.' Putting it most pointedly, Leslie Sehume said Nat was 'what we blacks would call a coconut' – that is to say, black on the outside, white on the inside.[2]

Too often, they complained, he seemed cozy with the middle-class white reformers whose approach to racial equality they found maddeningly slow and condescending. 'You can imagine, it was a very anti-white world we lived in,' said Joe Thloloe, 'and when we left the shebeens in town and went home to Soweto, there he was walking off to the [white] northern suburbs to spend time with Nadine Gordimer and her friends'.[3] As Nat wrote years later, he had never been able to convince himself that the white left was the true political enemy in South Africa. Even young Afrikaners earned his sympathy for being brainwashed into tacit acceptance of apartheid. 'In my view, my Afrikaner contemporaries are getting a raw deal,' he wrote. 'The grip of authority on the minds of black youth is not as tight as it is on theirs.'[4] This kind of rhetoric earned Nat a special distinction among some black friends and colleagues. 'Nat tommed,' said his colleague Wally Serote. 'He tommed while we were rat-racing for survival.'[5] To Serote and the others, Nat had refused to throw the force of his identity behind his blackness, and they couldn't understand why.

For many of Nat's friends and colleagues, the question was simple: how could any white person, no matter how sympathetic, begin to understand what life looked like on their side of the colour bar? Sure, white liberals sneaked into the townships to drink illegal liquor and listen to jazz music, to feel the energy and chaos that vibrated through that world and to see how the other 80 per cent lived. But at the end of the evening, they got into their cars and drove back into a different South Africa, one where the majority of children attended school, people held jobs that paid a living wage, and the sight of a policeman calmed the nerves rather than sent them racing. This South Africa had grocery stores and paved roads and libraries, and the people who lived there could vote, attend university and eat in restaurants.

Urban black intellectual life dazzled many of these left-leaning young whites because of the startling immediacy of its concerns and the rawness of its anger, qualities that felt distant, even among liberals, in the white world. But for black intellectuals themselves, the crucial distinction remained. However much a white South African bristled at apartheid's laws, however many nights she spent with her African boyfriend, she always woke up the next morning still white. The black urban world she experienced in snapshots made up the entirety of life for men like Nat. The same immediacy and rawness that thrilled his white friends held him in a chokehold. His circle drank voraciously, loved aggressively and balanced on the edge of the law not only because it was exciting, but because those in their social and racial position had no more stable path they could find their way onto – in short, no escape from their escapist life. How then, they wondered, could they stand shoulder to shoulder with whites politically? Even if they had the same goals, by the nature of the apartheid beast, blacks had to be scrappier, more radical and less compromising in the way they approached the issues.

But Nat never seemed to absorb that way of thinking completely. He'd grown up in a mixed township with a father committed to a multiracial strain of liberalism. His childhood was built on the idea that if you worked hard enough, behaved respectably enough and spoke sharply enough, the world would rise to meet your expectations – colour and class be damned. And even as he plunged into the *Drum* social world, he carried that sense of optimism with him. In that sense he was not so much a coconut as a chameleon – sometimes blending seamlessly with his scenery, but at other times vividly and suddenly out of place.

One day in the early years of *Drum*'s existence, a white painter came to the building to retouch the outer walls. He brought along a black assistant, and as the two began their work just outside the magazine's office, the boss began to berate his

A Native of Nowhere

employee, swearing at him and cursing his sloppy work. Finally, the assistant glanced inside at the black journalists sitting at their typewriters and muttered under his breath in Zulu, just loud enough for those inside to hear, 'You white man, you wish you could be in there doing that work, don't you?'[6]

That was the strange place of *Drum* in the apartheid ecosystem. Each day from his office, Nat looked out into downtown Johannesburg, watching as the miners and domestics who made up most of Johannesburg's black workforce trudged to and from work. 'I resented them,' he wrote, 'because I felt a responsibility towards them and I was doing nothing about it.'[7] Like the other *Drum* writers, he knew the rarity of his circumstance. In a country where more than two-thirds of African men could not even read, he had educated parents, several complete years of schooling and a knack for spinning magazine stories.[8] He never had to do a physical job more intense than delivering newspapers, and in his early twenties he had landed a spot on one of the only white-controlled payrolls that actually paid a living wage to its African employees. In a rare reversal of South Africa's racial hierarchy, he watched as white carpenters and painters did repairs in the *Drum* offices while he hammered out news articles. Looking into the streets of Johannesburg, Nat matched this existence against that of the black labourers, 'illiterate and doomed to stay that way for the rest of their lives' and felt a heavy sense of guilt.[9]

As intellectuals, Nat and his colleagues found themselves balancing on the edge of black society, aloof from the life of the African working class but at the same time distanced from white liberals by a chasm of rights and freedoms. *Drum*'s writers were members of the tiny African middle class, which meant simply that they maintained a degree of economic stability. Most of the *Drum* cadre, including Nat, had also received at least some secondary education from the country's mission-run black schools, an extreme rarity in a country where only half a per cent of all African men completed their 'matric', or high-school exit exams.[10] They didn't work long hours as miners or domestic servants, constantly teetering on the edge of unemployment, and they had white friends, an incalculable advantage in navigating the apartheid system. As the *Drum* writer Bloke Modisane explained, other Africans resentfully called intellectuals 'a Situation, something not belonging to either, but tactfully situated between white oppression and black rebellion'.[11] They carved out their intellectual niche, then, not merely to elude apartheid, but also to transcend the difficulties of working-class township life.

Nevertheless, the realities of black South Africa haunted them. Such a consciousness of the profound inequity in their country, which animated a tone of 'derisive laughter', 'implacable hatred' or 'self-corrosive cynicism' in the writing of Nat's *Drum* colleagues, led him instead to an even-handed and understated style – dispassionate, sympathetic and often subtly ironic.[12] His writings from the early years of his career in Johannesburg reveal the roving eye of a perceptive observer who cast his gaze across the breadth of what he called 'a clearly ugly town' and took it down in snapshots – a spat between rival gangs of taxi drivers, the brewing of illegal homemade liquors in the townships, the suicide of a popular boxer.[13]

A Native of Nowhere

Although the menace of the Suppression of Communism Act kept Nat and the other *Drum* writers from addressing racial politics head on, details of the personal impact of apartheid on black South Africans saturated their journalism. It didn't matter the subject of the article, from pop culture features to advice columns to news analysis, certain themes pervaded – race, discrimination, poverty, inequality. 'However much we tried to ignore them,' Anthony Sampson wrote, 'in South Africa all roads lead to politics.'[14] A piece by Nat on a successful black soccer team, for instance, made reference to their early lives in the 'slummy passages of Moroka'.[15] Even his profile of a cigar tycoon set him against 'the drabness of the Government-built township'.[16] Wherever you went in black society, it seemed, apartheid never lurked far from the edge of the frame.

Some time after Nat first went to work for *Drum*, he and the photographer Peter Magubane – whom he frequently worked with on stories – loaded up their gear and drove to Lobatse, Bechuanaland (now Botswana), where they were told they would find the Cape Town musicians Maud Damons and Spike Glasser. Days earlier, the couple had slipped out of South Africa to flee a charge under the Immorality Act, a nefarious law that prohibited sex and relationships across the colour line. Now, just across the border, they were plotting their future together, and Nat knew there'd be a story.

Huddled over beers in their hotel bar, he listened as Maud,

an olive-skinned coloured woman, and Spike, who was white, described their courtship. They had met through friends in the Cape Town music scene, she said, and started dating soon after. Spike had been drawn to her, he said, because she was 'the greatest jazz singer ever produced in South Africa'.[17] It was a love story so unremarkable as to be hardly worth commenting on, with one glaring exception: in South Africa it was criminal.

After a warrant was issued for their arrest, the couple conferred and decided to flee the country in secret. So one evening, Maud dropped her young son, Leroy, off at her mother's house, promising to pick him up after a singing gig at a local nightclub. Instead, she and Spike climbed into his car and pointed themselves north. Nineteen hours later, they were in Bechuanaland, a British protectorate that did not require entering South Africans to show passports. They would stay there, they told Nat, only until they could find a way into England, where they hoped to be able to pick up their musical careers again. 'Maud and I do not belong to any political party,' Spike griped. 'We are both extremely sorry to have left South Africa because we are both staunch patriots.'[18]

It is hard not to wonder what Nat thought as he scribbled down the couple's quotes or watched Spike casually lay his hand over Maud's. Over his years in Johannesburg, Nat developed a reputation – unsavoury to some – for being what his childhood friend Theo Zindela called 'addicted to white bread'. He was 'very keen on the white ladies', the photographer Alf Kumalo concurred. 'There was no secret about that – it was open.'[19]

In fact, white girlfriends were a common accessory in

Nat's circles, in part because having one did not simply ignore apartheid, it flaunted one's rejection of it. 'There is a law that says ... I cannot make love to a white woman,' Can once wrote. 'But stronger still there is a custom ... that shudders at the sheerest notion that any whiteman could contemplate, or any black man dare, a love affair across the colour line.' As he explained, he did not necessarily want to date white women – he simply wanted the right to.[20] The South African government, of course, had other ideas. Since 1927, the same Immorality Act that forced Maud and Spike out of South Africa had prohibited 'illicit carnal intercourse' between blacks and whites, a law the government extended in 1950 to include the vaguely defined category of 'all immoral or indecent acts'.[21] As in any racially charged society, however, the prohibition on interracial sex in South Africa ran deeper than legislation. It struck at the heart of racial identity in the country. To Nat, Can and the others, that gave breaking the taboo a particular charm.

But for all the memories people have of Nat's taste in women, almost nobody seems to remember the name of a single one of his white girlfriends. Indeed, during his early years in Johannesburg, there seem to be nearly no constant women in the frame at all. 'A *Drum* writer took sex and alcohol in his stride,' Lewis wrote.[22] Having a constant, changing supply of women at one's disposal became an integral part of the *Drum* persona. In their lives, as in their writing, women were beautiful, frivolous and plentiful, rarely allowed to play more than a bit part in the wider narrative.

'He had the white women of his choice,' said Peter

Magubane. 'Young, beautiful white women. It was a choice partly, to show everyone that apartheid doesn't work.' And Nat had his own quirky ways of winning their hearts. Nat wore a pair of beat-up old sandals, remembered his friend Roseinnes Phahle, the kind of shoes at which girls in the townships turned up their noses. They wanted something smarter, he said, something that showed you had a bit of money and a bit of style. But when Nat went off to visit white friends in the suburbs, suddenly he was the centre of attention, the object of fascination and just a hint of pity. 'They'd say to him, "Oh, how curious, how interesting,"' Rose said, 'and that's how he'd win them over.'[23]

But if it's impossible to know exactly who these white women were, it's much easier to think of places where he may have met them. Nat was a great connoisseur of the liberal suburban house party, where his crisp, nearly British accent and bad shoes played well to a crowd of white activists. Many of them took place at the Parktown home of Nadine Gordimer and her husband, the art dealer Reinhold Cassirer, which was by then a hub for the social life of the Johannesburg left.

Close to the University of the Witwatersrand and Sophiatown, their home on the tree-lined Frere Road was a place where a large circle of the city's writers and artists knew they could come to share a few drinks with a multiracial crowd. 'Reinhold had fled Nazi Germany,' Nadine said. 'And he said, "Why on earth have I left one fascist country to come to another?" He understood that certain risks were worth taking.' So they threw their parties, and they invited whom they wanted.

A Native of Nowhere

Like shebeen drinking, mixed parties thrown by white suburban couples were generally an ignorable offence to the Johannesburg police. 'You became an expert liar,' Nadine said. If the police came by, the black guests were your hired help, the drivers and gardeners and domestic workers that made the white South African world spin. And as soon as they left, the needle fell back on the record, the glasses of gin emerged from their hiding places, and the party continued. 'We were besieged – but we had our own strengths,' Nadine told me fifty years later. 'We knew who we were for and who we were against.'[24]

Drum's founder, Jim Bailey, was another frequent party host, ferrying his journalists off to his vast farm on the northern fringes of Johannesburg. In a secluded, tree-shrouded building they nicknamed Coney Island, the magazine's staff would stay up through the night dancing and playing music. Francie Suzman and Jim's future wife, Barbara – then a lanky 16-year-old – once tried to teach Nat to swim in the farmhouse pool, but to little effect. He was a useless pupil, just a flailing mass of leaden limbs, and the two finally threw their hands up in despair.[25] But mostly, Nat and the others came to Jim's house for long, rambling evenings secluded from the prying eyes of the South African police. As the nights sprawled towards morning and everyone grew bleary-eyed and silly drunk, Jim would drive his young charges back to the city, back to the townships, back to the places where they were technically allowed to be.

By all accounts, Nat was unapologetic about his taste for these suburban benders. 'Nat just lived the way he did. He didn't seem like he was trying to prove anything,' said his friend Willie Kgositsile. He took obvious pleasure in the mixed parties and the white women for the way they seemed to unsettle apartheid, but, more so than that, they were simply a way for him to slacken the restrictions placed on his own life. And many of the black writers and artists he worked with, if not embracing that lifestyle, certainly understood it. We teased him, Juby Mayet told me: 'You know, "Which larney [posh] chick were you with last night, Nat? Which larney house were you sleeping in?"' But it was never serious. Everyone had their way of surviving, she told me, and this was his.[26]

By the early 1960s, Nat had moved out of his place in Hillbrow and began renting a room in the Soweto neighbourhood of Orlando West, in a home owned by his friend Victor Sondlo. The house at No. 8348 was a standard-issue government building, squat, red brick, nearly identical to the houses on every side of it. Among township neighbourhoods, though, this was tops. Each of the houses in Orlando West had a fair-sized plot and a pit latrine at the back, and the suburb was orderly and full of families. Only a few miles away, in an almost identical house, lived the Mandela couple and their young children.

Directly in front of Victor's house stood one of the railway lines that carried black commuters from the township to the city each morning, and back each night. From their front veranda the two men would have seen the daily spectacle of

A Native of Nowhere

those trains: cars packed so tightly that passengers stood on the seats to make more room for incoming commuters. As the trains clacked along the tracks toward town, passengers clung desperately to the windows and door-frames from the outside.[27]

Beyond the tracks, Victor's house gazed out on the distinctive outline of two cooling towers. Hulking above the Soweto skyline, the towers ironically serviced the white metropolis to the north. The township itself did not have electricity, and wouldn't for another two decades. From the other side of the house, the view peered onto a stretch of flat-topped dusty yellow hills. These were the gold industry's crumbs, its mine dumps, the dust of decades of stripping out the long seam of gold that lay just beneath the city. The mine dumps were also, in a very literal sense, the dividing line between white and black Johannesburg, and a buffer zone between them. They rose out of the veld in massive, ugly domes of dust that kicked up into the air on windy days, sending a fine layer of yellow soot sprinkling down over the areas of Soweto closest to them. Each day as Nat drove his old car from Orlando West to Johannesburg, he would have passed these dumps. And each night from his house, he would have seen them from afar.

Was Nat a coconut, as his friend once called him? A black man with a "white" disposition? Perhaps – for whatever that meant. But he still lived on the dark side of South Africa's colour divide. No matter how much he sought to escape the system, there was no avoiding the physical boundaries being drawn around his life. The government had painted clean dark lines across the city – the mine dumps, the cooling towers, the township boundaries – landmarks to its own segregationist ingenuity. They meant that, however far someone like Nat walked into the white suburbs, however many nights he fell asleep on a suburban lawn, he would always end up back here, watching the dust rise over the mine dumps and the trains clattering homeward, carrying their passengers to the edges of a city in which they were only guests.

Four

ON THE MORNING OF 21 MARCH 1960, a mass of protesters and curious onlookers gathered in front of a police station in the township of Sharpeville, thirty miles south of Johannesburg. As part of a coordinated national campaign against the pass laws, the demonstrators had left their reference books at home, offering themselves up for arrest. But as the unarmed crowd continued to swell, the small contingent of policemen on duty at the station grew uneasy. Close to noon, they called in a fleet of armoured cars as back-up. When these failed to scare off the protesters, six air force fighter jets moved in, barrelling toward the crowd before swooping upward at the last moment. Still, the protesters refused to disperse.

Finally, at 1.20 p.m., an officer tried to grab a demonstrator positioned near the front of the crowd, and the group surged forward, flinging stones at the police. From above the din, police captain G.D. Pienaar shouted a warbled order and suddenly a shot rang out, then another. As the protesters fled in terror, bullets landed indiscriminately, reportedly felling a woman buying fruit from a vendor at the edge of the crowd, then a 10-year-old boy. In less than two minutes, at least 69 people lay dead and nearly 200 more wounded, most of them shot in the back as they ran from the police. 'I don't know how many we shot,' the police captain told a reporter soon after. 'My car was struck by a stone. If they do these things, they must learn their lesson the hard way.'[1]

The massacre at Sharpeville brought about a sharp shift in the relationship between anti-apartheid activists and the South African government. On 30 March the government declared a State of Emergency, granting itself wide-ranging powers to quell dissent. The following week, it banned both the ANC and the Pan Africanist Congress (PAC), which dealt a staggering blow to political organisers, forcing them to slip underground or out of the country. Shaken by the reality that police violence against passive resisters aroused no moral outrage from the South African government, both the ANC and the PAC launched campaigns of sabotage, primarily targeting government buildings and industrial sites. Although this tactic proved amateur and largely ineffective, it became a mainstay of protest technique in the coming years, a marker of the widening chasm between the state and its dissenters.

Sharpeville not only changed the tenor of apartheid resistance, it also dragged South Africa into the international spotlight. In April, the United Nations issued the first of several resolutions condemning South African human rights abuses and, later in the year, the ANC president, Albert Luthuli, received the Nobel Peace Prize for his work to end apartheid. 'Do the South Africans think that the rest of the world will

A Native of Nowhere

ignore such a massacre?' the *New York Times* demanded in an editorial.[2] Indeed, poking out from the bottom of a continent in the throes of dozens of independence movements, South Africa's white-controlled government began to look all the more anachronistic and self-destructive.[3]

Increased international attention on South Africa also brought with it a marked interest in the lives of the country's Africans. In late 1961, the *New York Times* magazine solicited an essay from Nat, which ran on 24 September beneath the headline 'The Human Meaning of Apartheid'. Flipping between reportage and personal narrative, the piece crafted an image of a country where, 'however distinguished an African may become, there is no hope of escaping his black skin'.[4] The prose, like most of Nat's oeuvre, was levelheaded and understated, preferring to describe scenes – a man being arrested for not having a pass book, a sign posted outside a government building declaring 'DOGS AND NATIVES NOT ALLOWED' – rather than directly puncture the apartheid apparatus.

But beneath the surface coursed a quiet rage. Describing the government's stated policies of separate, orderly development for each race, he demanded, 'is this why more than sixty Africans were shot dead … at Sharpeville last year?'[5] As he explained to his American readers, the National Party's façade of a neatly divided South Africa – one where white and black could live mutually exclusive existences – had torn the country apart from the inside out. Africans' own skin made them live in terror of the law, finding it increasingly difficult to escape the crushing weight of state-sanctioned oppression.

When Nat wrote of Africans' escalating fear and sense of powerlessness, his general language veiled just how close to home the issue had become for him as a writer. Already fearful of a government crackdown, in the State of Emergency after Sharpeville *Drum* faced two stark options: either to severely limit its political content or be banned completely by the government. The state's emergency regulations blocked the magazine's staff from publishing their account of the shooting for more than six months.[6] The May 1960 issue of *Drum* – the first to go to press after the tragedy – featured only a photographic spread of the funerals held for Sharpeville victims, headlined by a stark image of a long line of coffins and mourners, both of them trailing out to the edge of the frame.[7] And in the July issue, Nat reported on a cadre of ANC activists involved with the anti-pass campaigns who had gone into exile in Basutoland (now Lesotho). In the 1,500 words of the piece, he never mentioned the word 'Sharpeville'.[8] Forced into a kind of journalistic amnesia, Nat and *Drum* struggled to convey the magnitude of apartheid resistance in a country whose rulers were intent on pretending it did not exist.

This chokehold around the country's news intensified a problem already building in the *Drum* offices – retaining writers in a country that refused to let them write. Over the previous three years, the sardonic former *Drum* editor Sylvester Stein, who helped Nat get his first pass in Johannesburg, as well as writers and friends Todd Matshikiza, Arthur Maimane and Bloke Modisane, slipped into exile in Europe, unwilling to continue living subversively in the country of their birth. With the government and police hovering low over the activities of dissidents, the antics of fringe country began to feel for many as if they simply were not worth the tremendous danger they posed.

For Nat's closest friends, too, the prospects of life abroad were beginning to tug at their resolve to stay and write in South Africa. In early 1960, Nat and Lewis had met an American academic named Jack Thompson, who was passing through Johannesburg on a literary tour of Africa. The two men had plucked him from a white suburban dinner party, which Lewis grumbled they'd been invited to as kind of 'mascots' for the black literary scene, and took him out for a night in the Soweto shebeens. Over Castle Milk Stouts, Lewis and Nat listened as Jack explained to them that he ran a philanthropic organisation called the Farfield Foundation, which bankrolled artistic and cultural projects around the world. The group was looking to fund a black South African writer to come to Harvard University as a Nieman fellow – a prestigious year-long journalism programme at the university. Did Nat and Lewis know of anyone who might be interested?

The next morning, as Jack 'carried with him into the plane to Ghana a man-sized hangover', Lewis took stock of the idea. The fellowship would connect him to some of the best journalists in the world, and it was a chance to see the world beyond apartheid's bounds. 'It would be wonderful to read literature for a year, and be able to write without the pressure of earning a living,' he wrote to Francie Suzman in May.[9] So, he decided, he would apply. And within months, he and Jack had finalised his fellowship. All that was left was to apply for a passport.

In this application process, Lewis was joined by Aubrey Sussens, the white editor of the liberal *Rand Daily Mail* and the other South African awarded a Nieman fellowship that year. But when the two men sent in their passport forms, the results diverged strangely. While Aubrey's application went through immediately, Lewis waited for months. Finally, in September 1961, he learned that he had been denied.[10]

Lewis, however, had determined he would get out. 'All the good people seem to be always leaving for elsewhere,' he wrote to Francie.[11] So he turned to a friend for help, the Marxist lawyer and sociologist Harold Wolpe. Sifting through the statute books, Harold discovered an 'exit permit clause' in the 1955 Departure from the Union Regulation Act, the law that outlined the regulations for citizen entry to and exit from the country. The clause, he surmised, allowed the bearer to exit the country without a passport, but with a brutal caveat – he or she could never return. The exit permit, in effect, rendered its users entirely stateless. But Lewis recognised that if he wanted a chance at a life without the grip of apartheid, he had little choice. He decided to leave behind Johannesburg, Nat and the *Drum* world and take the one-way ticket.[12]

On the day Lewis left for the United States, Nat accompanied him to the Johannesburg airport. There, in the crowded terminal, the two friends did what they had always done when faced with the absurdities of apartheid, the same thing they had done that autumn morning at the Texan years before – they clowned. 'This is it,' Lewis said, 'from now on I'm a full fledged roving journalist.'[13] Both men knew, however, that the task of staying afloat as a black South African writer was no longer a laughing matter. In the short time they had been in Johannesburg, they had watched the veneer of black intellectual culture chip away, with the dynamism and relative openness of a world coloured by Sophiatown giving way to a police state set against the backdrop of Sharpeville.

In the city where both men had grown up intellectually, socially and artistically, the blistering pace of black urban life had begun to catch up with those who lived it. In the shadow of March 1960, the loose, bravado-powered community they had built in illegal drinking holes and multiracial parties found itself ill-equipped to face off against organised state repression and, increasingly, its members ran for higher ground, slipping into exile across Africa, Europe and the United States.

For some, however, the twilight of the fringe country that Nat had once described in a *Drum* article lingered. Nat had not yet been banned or arrested, and his skilled reportage had catapulted his name all the way onto the pages of the *New York Times*. He still had something to hold onto in South Africa, and no real desire to leave the only country he had ever known. So that day in the airport, he said his goodbyes to Lewis and headed home to Soweto. Fringe country was slipping away, but he would stay behind to make sense of what was left.

By late 1961, *Drum* too had reached a crossroads. Nearly as soon as Lewis left for the United States, the magazine's editor-in-chief, a sharp-featured Englishman named Tom Hopkinson, handed in his own resignation. During the previous several months, he had clashed repeatedly with *Drum*'s owner, Jim Bailey, over how the magazine should be run and what it should contain. After the government imposed a State of Emergency following the March 1960 protests, Jim insisted that the magazine feature 'much less serious and much less political stuff', and instead focus its energies on stories of township life. But Tom found that policy unsettling and unproductive. 'It was dull work editing a magazine in which virtually nothing could be said,' he griped. So he said his goodbyes to his staff, remarking to Nat that during his three years at *Drum*, he had become 'fit to work on any paper in the world', and headed out.[14]

The magazine Tom Hopkinson left behind looked much the same as the one on which Nat had taken a job in 1958. Elegant, voluptuous women still graced each month's cover. The pages still detailed the lives of township 'witch doctors', the rise and fall of popular sports teams, and the romantic problems of readers ('Can't a fat man find love?'), alongside features on politics and revolution across the continent. But there were subtle differences as well. More and more of the political articles focused on international news – protests in Southern Rhodesia, Ghana's foreign policy, the independence of Tanganyika (later, Tanzania).[15] Many pieces on South Africa itself were little more than transcriptions of interviews with black leaders, with *Drum*'s opinion – and often even the name of the reporter – well concealed.[16] After Sharpeville, the magazine began to consult with lawyers before any controversial story went to press, hacking off sections deemed likely to stir up trouble with the police, and the editors were increasingly careful to appear balanced in their reporting. A January 1961 piece on peasants' revolts in the 'native reserve' of Pondoland, for example, featured a large sidebar with the clunky title 'Here is the government's point of view', and in June, a Q&A with ANC and PAC leaders regarding upcoming anti-government protests also included responses from several National Party figureheads. As Jim Bailey saw it, the magazine had the responsibility simply to stay alive, not risk a confrontation with an increasingly merciless government.[17]

With *Drum* adjusting and readjusting its lens on South African politics, Nat received one of his most ambitious reporting assignments to date. Joined by the photographer Peter Magubane, a frequent reporting companion, and the white writer Dick Walker, he set off in mid-1961 to report on living conditions in South West Africa, the sprawling South African-controlled appendage which later became independent as Namibia. The territory no doubt interested *Drum*, as it did the international community, in part because it provided a bizarre tangent in the narrative of African independence. In 1961, as African states severed ties with their colonial rulers – or, in the case of South Africa, tightened their grip – South West Africa existed in a fuzzy legal space, recognised formally as neither a colony nor an independent state. The South African government ruled the territory ostensibly under a former League of Nations mandate, a legal proceeding established after World War I to transfer colonial holdings of the defeated parties into new hands.[18] But by 1961, any territorial agreement drawn up by the League

85

of Nations was an evident anachronism, and South Africa's refusal to acquiesce in the UN's more stringent demands for trusteeship meant that it clung tenuously to its legitimacy as a ruling power.

From the Johannesburg offices of *Drum*, Nat had watched the South African government and the UN lob ineffectual demands regarding South West African sovereignty back and forth across the negotiating table, achieving little besides mutual suspicion and irritation. Finally, in July, South Africa flatly refused entry to the UN Committee on South West Africa, threatening to arrest the group if it stepped onto South African-controlled soil. *Drum* immediately took its cue. With international diplomats barred, South African journalists were uniquely placed to report on happenings within the country. The editors dispatched Nat, Dick and Peter, and on 2 August they set out on the 12-hour drive to the South West African border.[19]

That evening, the three men passed into the country and, as darkness fell on the scrubby brush, pulled into a filling station. 'That was our first blunder,' Nat later wrote. The multiracial group caught the eye of one of the attendants and soon the three men were sitting face to face with two policemen at the local precinct. But their passes, the officers realised, were all in order, and they were forced to let the men go. 'Half this place is just desert,' Nat remarked when they were on the road again. 'Cops and desert,' Peter corrected.[20]

Four hundred miles further on, in the capital city of Windhoek, the three men stopped again, and Nat and Peter broke off from their white companion. In a familiar mould,

A Native of Nowhere

South West African cities were carefully segregated, and it only made sense for the reporters to tread on their own race's trail. Over the next four days, Nat moved from township to township, interviewing residents on a subject he himself knew quite well – life as an African under National Party rule. Indeed, the poverty he described in South West Africa had the distinct flair of apartheid, with the same communities of migrant labourers who worked away from home for eleven months each year, the same terror that one's township would be suddenly marked for 'slum clearance'. As he had tea in the shacks of widows whose husbands had been killed by the police, or drove through the parched 'reserves' that made up the majority of black rural land in the country, Nat stared down a frank truth – apartheid South Africa had broken free of its own borders.

When Nat returned to Johannesburg, he wrote two pieces based on his trip, which appeared in the September and October 1961 issues of *Drum*. Their criticism of the situation in South West Africa, as per the magazine's style, was muted, cased in the particularities of individual experiences rather than presented as a broad social critique. But even that kind of writing had become increasingly consequential. Although it is unclear if Nat knew it, the South African police had tailed him to Windhoek, reporting that he 'went looking for locations' (townships) and 'connected with left-leaning people'.[21] As Jim Bailey had warned, black writers could keep working in Johannesburg, but only if they learned to keep their heads down.

But Nat pushed forward. In mid-1962, he and Peter drove

to Mozambique, one of the few countries where the white grip on power seemed just as strong as it was in South Africa. The previous year, the Portuguese colonial government had rounded up most of the country's sizeable Indian minority and herded them into internment camps, a move to force India to free 3,000 prisoners it had captured in its annexation of the Portuguese island of Goa the previous year. When Nat and Peter arrived, they were eking out a life behind barbed wire, resigned and patient. One night, the two men returned to their hotel room to find several rolls of film exposed and spoiled in their room. 'That was never explained,' Nat wrote. 'But neither were many other things.'[22]

And then there was the case of Philip Kgosana, a political exile whom Nat met in the hinterlands of Basutoland. The week after Sharpeville, the 23-year-old had briefly captured international attention when he led a march of 30,000 Africans through downtown Cape Town. After police convinced him not to march on Parliament, where he planned to demand a meeting with the Minister of Justice, Philip had taken the demonstrators to the city's police headquarters. There, dressed in shorts and looking every bit his young age, he demanded to meet with the Minister of Justice. After deliberating, the police commandant agreed, so long as Philip agreed to send home the chanting throng behind him. The young man paused. Should he defy the request, let the crowd surge forward into downtown Cape Town and offer themselves up for arrest? The marchers, after all, were poised to move on his command. 'When I told them to sit down, they sat down,' he later testified. 'When I ordered them to go back quietly, they went back quietly.' At Philip's behest, the march quietly crumbled, but the government never had any intention of holding up its end of the deal. When he returned for his meeting with the minister, he was summarily arrested.

The following year, as he awaited trial, he'd fled the country and ended up in the backcountry of Basutoland. That was where Nat found him, hiding out with a friend in the mountains far from the capital city of Maseru, where the South African authorities were searching for him. 'The only newspaper man I have talked to,' Philip announced proudly in the April 1962 edition of *Drum*, 'was … Nat Nakasa. I have told him my whole story.'

But what he told Nat was hardly encouraging for a young writer trying to swim against apartheid's tide. 'From now on,' Philip said, 'I'm silent.' He couldn't risk any more press exposure that might reveal his hand to the South African authorities, who had been circling him from afar since he left the country. Leaving South Africa had been the only option. 'If I had stayed any longer I was sure to be destroyed,' he told Nat evenly. 'I sincerely believe that, one way or the other, I would have been killed.'[23]

A half-century later, Philip still remembers Nat coming to visit him, his wheezing old car trundling up Basutoland's untarred roads. He'd met Nat once before, in Johannesburg, and was struck most of all by how young he was – no older than Philip himself, and 'very brave and tough'. The two men settled down at Philip's kitchen table to talk about his escape from South Africa as Peter Magubane circled them, snapping photographs. Philip told Nat that he was trying to find a place that would take him permanently. This business of fleeing your country was logistically complicated, he explained. You had no passport, no visas. All you could hope to do was beg a place in another country. Maybe, he thought, England would take him. That day, Philip said, 'Nat was not a talkative guy.'[24] He seemed thoughtful, serious. Perhaps that was because these were not simply idle considerations for him. After all, the question of leaving home was becoming desperately personal.

Five

IN EARLY 1962, NAT GATHERED together a group of friends at his favourite shebeen, the Classic. Despite growing state repression, despite the increased danger of living – let alone writing – in South Africa, that night the young journalist was buoyant. Drinks, he announced to his friends, were on him. As the men gladly drained their glasses of beer, Nat told the group that he had brought them together to discuss an idea. '[At that time] ideas were sprouting all over the place,' remembered Can, 'but any excuse for a drink was good enough.'[1] This particular idea, however, caught his ear. Nat Nakasa, 24 years old and never educated in literature beyond a basic high-school primer, wanted to start his own literary magazine.

Enough, he said, of talented African writers playing second-best to internationally renowned white South African novelists like Alan Paton and Nadine Gordimer. Black writers could speak to their own experiences, in their own voices. Just as *Drum* had given a megaphone to a generation of urban

African journalists, so a literary magazine could do the same for poets and novelists. But of course the ethic of the magazine, in true Nat fashion, would be one of inclusion. Black, white, coloured, Indian – if you could call yourself a citizen of the African continent, there was a place for your talent in his imagined publication. And for a name? 'For want of superior inspiration,' Can wrote, 'we decided to call the damned thing *The Classic*.'[2]

Over the next two years, the magazine that saw its genesis that night in the smoky bar took its place among the pre-eminent black literary endeavours in the country, attracting an international cadre of writers, subscribers and funders. But as National Party rule tightened in response to the massive wave of protest rising against it in the late 1950s, the very act of being both black and pre-eminent posed an increasing threat to the established social order. By the time Nat founded *The Classic*, apartheid had leached so far into the lives of South Africans that nearly every decision an individual made, from where they lived to the books they read to the people they slept with, could be a dissident act – especially if they fell on the wrong side of the colour line. And literary production was no exception. With state censorship advancing to snuff out black expression in the early 1960s, the lines between the literary and the political blurred, until the very act of writing as an African became its own form of protest activity. As Nat asserted, *The Classic* was 'as non-political as the life of a domestic servant, the life of a Dutch Reformed Church predikant [minister] or that of an opulent Johannesburg business man', in other words, impossibly, unavoidably political, caught – like its young editor – in the crossfire of a country at war with itself.[3]

Indeed, the space for black writers in apartheid South Africa shrank rapidly in the early 1960s. In the aftermath of Sharpeville, the state took measured aim at dissidents of all stripes, including journalists, muzzling them with censorship and bans on publishing. For political activists, the situation proved even grimmer. A single trial in 1963–4 brought down nearly all of the country's most prominent anti-apartheid activists, sending them to prison for life in a desolate island jail off the coast of Cape Town. As many other activists slipped underground or into exile, an eerie silence descended over the protest movement. But this time, the wise-cracking, fast-living antics of the country's black writers could do little to plug the gap. Nat struggled to fill the pages of *The Classic* with quality writers who had not yet been prohibited from writing in South Africa, while *Drum* also slipped into survival mode, sanitising its content to fly low under the radar of government surveillance. With many of its founding writers and editors now abroad, the magazine limped into the mid-1960s, a shell of its former self.

Underlying much of the writers' fear was a single, bizarrely powerful word: 'communist'. Since the inception of National Party rule, the apartheid government had hurled the term at its opponents with nearly indiscriminate fury, regardless of their affiliation with an actual communist party or ideological alignment with Marxist principles. In fact, the 1950 Suppression of Communism Act cast so wide a net in defining communism that dissidents could be slapped with the label for committing any act that sought to bring about 'political, industrial, social or economic change' within the country.[4] With the Cold War escalating in the early 1960s, the word 'communist' had become little more than a weapon of blunt force in the battle against protesters and activists, aimed promiscuously at anyone who challenged the government's authority.

The National Party's anti-communist fervour slashed through the South African writing community, eventually coming to rest on Nat himself. But ironically, by the time the government prepared to ban him as a communist in 1964 for 'stimulation of the spirit of hostility between the whites and non-whites', Nat had become for the United States government a bulwark in the struggle *against* communism.[5] Although he didn't know it, the American cultural organisation that funded the initial run of *The Classic* was bankrolled by the American Central Intelligence Agency (CIA) as part of a global effort to build a non-communist intellectual community in the 'third world'. American politicians harboured a deep fear that African independence movements – including the anti-apartheid struggle in South Africa – would give birth to a spate of new communist nations, and in response they offered support to both the National Party government and seemingly moderate opposition figures like Nat. Thus, by the time the young writer reached his mid-twenties, two governments had developed a vested and conflicting interest in his relationship to an ideology that he had never either claimed or denied.

Amidst all of the tremendous uncertainty Nat faced in the early 1960s, however, the period was also marked by a momentous rise in his own career. With the size of South

Africa's black intellectual community shrinking, the young writer skyrocketed through its ranks. In a three-year span between 1961 and 1964, he not only founded a literary magazine and continued to write for *Drum*, but also became the first black columnist for the leading liberal white newspaper, the *Rand Daily Mail*. By the time he was 26 years old, he had been invited to follow Lewis Nkosi to the United States on a prestigious journalism fellowship at Harvard University. But if the South African government appeared determined to purge itself of dissident intellectual activity, it also sought to contain those same intellectuals within its own borders. So as Nat turned his sights to the United States, he came up against a government intent on keeping him firmly rooted in the country of his birth.

When Nat gathered his friends together that night at the Classic, he had little idea of what would go into running a literary magazine. But he had been in Johannesburg for more than four years, enough time to recognise that black literary production in the city had few outlets. For novelists in particular, publication proved a daunting prospect. The labour-intensive process of bringing a book to life, from editing to printing to advertising and distribution, required the financial backing of a white publishing house. But liberal English-language presses were practically nonexistent in South Africa. With the government throwing its support behind Afrikaans as the language of arts and culture, prominent English-language writers had long looked to London for publication opportunities, short-circuiting both the South African publishing industry and the country's penchant for literary censorship. This meant that for black writers to be able to publish a novel or similar work in the 1960s, they had to have strong international connections and know how to appeal to a largely European audience. 'The African is constantly aware that if his short story, novel or play is ever going to be published or performed, it must make sense to white people,' explained the *Drum* writer Arthur Maimane.[6] In these conditions, few black South African writers managed to get projects off the ground, and book-length literary publication fizzled.

With publishing houses largely out of reach, magazines remained the sole remaining option open to most black creative writers. But aside from a few sporadically published literary journals and a handful of left-wing political magazines that accepted fiction, there were few places that even published short stories and poetry.[7] As Nat intended it, *The Classic* would step in and help fill this niche, publishing quarterly a collection of stories and poems written by Africans, a term he took broadly to mean anyone from the African continent, regardless of race or exile status.[8]

But before the magazine expanded into anything more than an idea, it hit its first snag – cash flow. A group of young writers barely scraping together enough for their own lives was hardly an ideal group to back a literary magazine financially. So they turned abroad for funding, to the United States. Nat wrote to Jack Thompson, the American academic with whom he and Lewis had got drunk in the Soweto shebeens two years earlier.

The professor was an enthusiastic patron of African writing, and when Nat asked if his Farfield Foundation would be interested in backing the new project, he immediately said yes. In May 1962, Farfield pledged $1,600 to the initial one-year run of *The Classic*, setting in motion Nat's literary ambitions.[9]

Beneath the surface of Jack's enthusiastic support for Nat, however, lay a powerful secret. The Farfield Foundation, which Nat knew only from Thompson and the group's minimalist stationery, described its mission as to 'preserv[e] the cultural heritage of the free world' by funding literary, artistic and scientific enterprises that strengthened 'the cultural ties that bind nations'.[10] But what the organisation did not say, and, indeed, what few outside its board of directors knew, was that Farfield received its funding directly from the CIA.

Although Jack seems never to have informed Nat, Farfield was part of a constellation of philanthropic 'organisations' – in reality little more than letterheads and bank accounts – that the CIA developed in the 1950s and 1960s to cultivate a pro-American intellectual elite throughout the West and the non-aligned world. As the agency's now infamous covert political operations against communism drew the world's gaze, the CIA also funnelled millions of dollars into the development of cultural and intellectual institutions – magazines, journals, concerts, movies, conferences, music festivals – that it believed could lock horns with the writers, artists and theorists emerging from the Eastern bloc.[11] Like much of the CIA's work during the Cold War, its cultural programmes had nebulous and diffuse purposes, providing money for everything from Jackson Pollock paintings to Lebanese literary magazines to a Parisian run of Stravinsky's *Rite of Spring*.[12] The recipients were united only by the perceived ability of their funding to conjure up good will for American interests and to promote a vaguely defined non-communist worldview.

In Africa, these cultural overtures against communism held special significance. As countries across the continent came unmoored from their former colonial powers by the dozens in the early 1960s, the United States feared that any of these new nations could be a new communist nation – allying not only its politics but also its military, markets and labour with the Soviet Union. With the ideology of communism so deeply rooted in revolution, US foreign policy experts believed that if it became mixed with the nationalism sweeping Africa, a wide communist takeover on the continent was a real possibility. Building a moderate intellectual elite interested in stability and reform as opposed to open rebellion was thus seen as a crucial move to prevent this fate.[13]

Guided by this belief, Jack Thompson and Farfield sought to create a community of literary intellectuals across Africa. Surveying the political landscape of the continent, Thompson later said that he had been struck in several cases by the importance of 'literary people' in the transition from colony to nation.[14] The most obvious example of this trend was the acclaimed French-language poet Léopold Senghor, who became Senegal's first post-independence president in 1960. In Senghor and the rest of the African literary elite, Jack saw the possibility of a stable transition to democracy, marked not by violence but by dialogue. Given this overarching mission, Nat's own particular politics were of little importance to

Thompson, and the funding for *The Classic* came with 'no strings attached whatsoever'.[15] Nat was simply seen as an anchor, holding black cultural expression steady as the politics of liberation churned around it.

As Farfield set Nat's magazine financially in motion, the newly appointed editor had little idea just what running a literary magazine meant. Still working full-time for *Drum*, Nat's responsibilities at *The Classic*, from building a staff to finding a publisher to seeking worthy submissions, began to snowball. In December 1962, Jack expressed his delight that *The Classic* was 'at last ready to go into production', but as the new year began, the magazine failed to materialise, and the funders grew increasingly anxious.[16] In February 1963, Lewis chastised his friend for falling out of touch with Thompson. 'It wasn't nice to get letters ... from Jack saying he hadn't heard a word from you and didn't know what was happening,' he wrote.[17] Shape up, he told Nat, or this chance would soon be gone.

Throughout the autumn, Nat took heed of this advice, sending a flurry of letters to friends and colleagues soliciting submissions and asking for advice on the content. His repeated calls for counsel and criticism reveal the doubts he felt about his own literary background, which consisted of little more than his high-school English courses. As he explained to Lewis, judging pieces for *The Classic* meant he was beefing up his knowledge of literature more generally, 'which you know I need desperately to do'.[18] As Lewis would recall a decade later, Nat was in many ways a curious editor for a literary magazine. 'I put books his way to read and was often frustrated by his singular lack of interest,' he wrote. 'He seemed to be someone who wanted to absorb life directly.'[19]

Nadine Gordimer, who sat on *The Classic*'s founding board, echoed this sentiment, noting that he wasn't well read and she often had the difficult task of informing him 'that some poems he considered publishing in the magazine were rubbish'.[20] But Nadine also remembered that Nat relished the process of learning how to tell the difference. Sitting in the sunny living room of her Parktown house, their papers splayed across the floor, the two spent long hours inspecting submissions to the magazine. Nadine was fourteen years Nat's senior, already an internationally established writer, and she says she could see that Nat was headed in that direction as well. Indeed, they became so close that some speculated that it was far more than a professional relationship. But it seems more likely that Nat had simply become like a member of the family. When he came by from the *Drum* office, Nadine would call ahead to ask him to bring a bottle of milk, or to collect her son at the bus stop. 'We would eat bread and cheese on the verandah in the sun, laughing a lot ... and getting on with the work at the same time,' she wrote. As mentor and mentee, they were drawn even closer together by *The Classic*.

As he sifted through potential content, Nat also struggled to nail down some of the less tangible aspects of running a literary magazine. He had to deal with printers unused to working with black writers, who peppered him with pedantic questions and referred to him as 'boy'.[21] Would-be contributors repeatedly sent him several letters before receiving a breathless and apologetic response, and he frequently circumvented a particularly important question. 'Presumably I'm going to be paid for my contributions,' wrote an incredulous Can Themba, who had submitted a story to the first issue. 'If so, when? If not, why the bloody hell not?'[22] Arthur Maimane was even more pointed with the young editor. 'What you need is a correspondence course on How to Persuade Authors and Keep Them Contributing,' he wrote. 'You don't just ignore potential contributors as rudely as you do, between demands to them for stories.'[23] Joe Thloloe, on the other hand, remembered receiving from Nat one of the kindest rejections of his life. When he decided he didn't want the story, he'd called Joe and invited him to sit and talk about it. The two carefully surveyed the piece, with Nat noting the weaknesses that had kept it out of the 'yes' pile.[24]

The first issue of *The Classic* finally arrived in print in June 1963 with an initial run of 1,500 copies. After Nat's mad scramble for submissions, the opening issue featured stories and poems from several rising South African literary stars, including Can, Es'kia Mphahlele and Casey Motsisi, a realisation of Nat's promise in his editor's note that the magazine would be a home for 'African writing of merit'. At home and abroad, the South African intellectual community fêted the magazine's release, although complaints confirmed the worries of Nadine and Lewis – the selection of content left something to be desired. In *Information and Analysis: South Africa*, a monthly bulletin on South African news published by a group of exiles living in Paris, Richard Rive wrote that the magazine was 'healthy enough' but there was much that was 'mediocre and plain bad' in the first issue. But Es'kia assured

Nat that, whatever the deficiencies the first issue contained, it was a 'good and worthy beginning'.[25]

The Americans writing the cheques also seemed pleased, and by the end of the winter Nat had quit his job at *Drum* to run *The Classic* full-time on a salary from Farfield. As Nadine would later remember, Nat had come into his own working on the magazine and had developed an editorial style that was 'serious and yet light-handed, gay, candid and unflustered'.[26] The second issue was released in November, to far more encouraging reviews, and he began to turn his sights to Francophone and Lusophone Africa to assemble issues featuring translated works for the following year.

Although *The Classic* was not the only journal of English-language creative writing in South Africa at the time of its publication, it quickly developed a unique and important identity within the country's literary landscape. Among the small crop of literary magazines making the rounds in the early 1960s – *Contrast* and *The Purple Renoster* ('The Purple Rhinoceros') prominent among them – it was only *The Classic* that ever developed a reputation for being particularly receptive to black prose. Indeed, the tables of contents for many of the other magazines from the same era read like a who's who of white South African writers, publishing stories and poems from the likes of Barney Simon, Nadine Gordimer, Ingrid Jonker and Athol Fugard – with a black writer appearing perhaps every year or two for a bit of added diversity. *The Classic*, on the other hand, was dominated by black writers.

Perhaps because of this enthusiasm for black African writing, Nat's magazine also openly embraced the intrinsic entanglement of the literary and the political. As he wrote in his first editor's note, 'If the daily lives [of our contributors] are not regulated by political decisions, that will be reflected in *The Classic*. If, however, the work they do, if their sexual lives and their search for God are governed by political decrees, then that will also be reflected in the material published by *The Classic*. After all, these stories and poems and drawings and sculpture will be about the lives of these people.'[27] So evident were the political undertones in the first issue of *The Classic* that Jack Thompson chastised Nat for neglecting writing quality in favour of flouting the government. 'Your poems seem to me often to be more concerned with making a statement than with making a poem,' he wrote in August 1963.[28] But that statement ignored a basic fact of Nat's undertaking: to make a poem in apartheid South Africa, particularly as a black writer, was to make a statement in and of itself.

Although it had neither the reach nor the influence of a popular glossy magazine like *Drum*, *The Classic* exposed those who wrote for it to another important audience: other writers. From their overlapping tables of contents and conversational editor's notes, it is evident that South Africa's small literary magazines did not exist in isolation, but formed a kind of knot tethering the country's community of writers together.[29] Many who made their earliest forays into professional writing through literary magazines like *The Classic* would go on to become nationally and internationally recognised figures. Wally Serote, later one of South Africa's leading poets, was 21 years old when he first picked up a copy of *The Classic*, and it was a revelation. 'I had done my matric and I had been trained in English, but nearly everything I'd read was European literature,' he said. 'It never occurred to me that you could write about Africans.'[30] Poring over an issue of the magazine that he had stolen from the University of the Witwatersrand's library, Wally saw his own future written in its pages.

Indeed, what set *The Classic* apart from other magazines of its time was that it forced into publication a vision of a different South Africa. Although the magazine would go on in its later issues to feature writing by international notables including Doris Lessing and Léopold Senghor, South African writing always remained especially important to Nat and the other editors. As Barney Simon, who later took the reins as editor-in-chief, explained, the magazine was meant to be a reservoir of 'the textures ... the aliveness, the sense of corrugated iron, concrete, flesh, sweat and heat that is Johannesburg'.[31] In this sense *The Classic*, like Nat's other writing endeavours, was an exercise in literary self-preservation. As the landscape and culture of Johannesburg shifted under the whims of state-enforced segregation, he found a way to stop the clock, freezing his version of the city in time through art, and writing and exporting this vision to an international audience.

Just as *The Classic* kicked into gear, however, Nat began to express a deep irritation with life in South Africa, repeatedly complaining to friends and colleagues that he 'felt like hopping on the next plane to go seek my fortune outside

A Native of Nowhere

this hole'. Even fringe country had lost its sheen. One night the playwright and director Barney Simon invited Nat to a party at the house of an English academic they both knew. The parties were a regular occurrence, and Nat often dropped in, but that evening, Barney remembered, the gathering was particularly raucous. 'People were twisting wildly, singing with the record at the top of their voices,' he wrote, 'heads were thrown back, bodies bounced against one another.' Nat took one look at the scene, re-buttoned his coat and wheeled around to leave. When Barney tried to pull him back in, he snapped, asking if his friend realised that 'most of the blacks we were carousing with were dangerous gangsters and whores'.[32] On another occasion, Nat introduced Barney to a writer he had just published in *The Classic*, a former gangster and general rabble-rouser named Dugmore Boetie. Barney remembered being fascinated by the man, 'relishing all the rogue that showed', but Nat, 'sophisticated, urbane, was irritated by him'.[33] To Barney, Nat appeared to have lost his patience for the dangerous and often limited world he and his friends inhabited. He was restless, and he wanted out.

Nat's frustration with fringe country was compounded by the growing danger of publishing literature in South Africa. In the autumn of 1963, he was forced to reject a short story submitted to *The Classic* because it was 'too hot to handle because [of] a rather bold bedroom angle', which Nat realised could catch the eye of the government censors and could spell death to the entire magazine.[34] Anything the National Party didn't want in print, it had the power to keep out of the public's reach, and he knew it.

That same year, Parliament had passed the Publications and Entertainment Act, a piece of legislation that, much like the Suppression of Communism Act, granted the state broad powers to ban or censor content it deemed unfavourable. This time around, the list included anything that was 'harmful to public morals', blasphemous, ridiculed 'any section of the inhabitants of the Republic', or posed a danger to the general peace.[35] The targets, simply put, were politics, sex and blasphemy. While many anti-apartheid writings naturally fell victim to this law, it also ensnared a vast number of other publications, among them Shirley Jackson's 'The Lottery' and Vladimir Nabokov's *Lolita*, eventually resulting in the censorship of a staggering 15,000 books and newspapers.[36] In 1964 an issue of the leftist political magazine *The New African* was banned ostensibly on the grounds of a single phrase contained within it – 'shit-scared'.[37] For editors like Nat, it was nearly impossible to know what would trip the wires and catch the government's attention.

As censorship slowly advanced, it collided with a vicious new wave of political oppression, underscoring the fundamental danger of any action that challenged National Party authority. On 11 July 1963, several of the anti-apartheid movement's highest-ranking leaders met to talk strategy for the sabotage campaign at Lilliesleaf Farm, a secluded safe house ten miles north of Johannesburg in an area called Rivonia. With so many activists jailed, the group knew that it was only a matter of time before the Rivonia location leaked, and this was to be their last business meeting at the farm. But as the men sat down around the Lilliesleaf dining-room table, they heard the

A Native of Nowhere

sounds of a van approaching from the main road. They always knew whom to expect at the farm – the foreign vehicle could mean only one thing.

The police raid at Rivonia captured a total of nineteen activists, among them several members of the ANC's senior leadership. The human cost was devastating, but the raid's impact did not end there. In their search of the property, the police collected a trove of incriminating documents, which revealed the ANC's planned sabotage campaign in meticulous detail. Together, the arrests and the discovery of the documents proved enough to sentence eight prominent anti-apartheid leaders to life in prison, including the charismatic young lawyer and ANC leader, Nelson Mandela, who had been jailed on a lesser charge since the previous year. The blow fractured the already hobbled resistance movement. Coupled with the arrest of the PAC president Robert Sobukwe in 1960 and the banning or house arrest of dozens of other leaders, after the Rivonia raid there was a virtually complete vacuum of anti-apartheid leadership within South Africa itself. By 1965, more than 8,000 people had been charged with crimes connected to 'political defiance', and nearly fifty sentenced to death. Resistance figures who had not yet been arrested fled into exile. In prison on Robben Island, off the coast of Cape Town, the once vibrant leaders of the resistance began to fade from view, consigned to a life of hard labour far from the public eye.

For writers too, the danger of life in South Africa was escalating. As if to underscore the closing space between politics and literature, the activists convicted in the Rivonia trial had asked Alan Paton, acclaimed author of the novel *Cry, the Beloved Country*, and founder of the anti-apartheid Liberal Party, to speak on their behalf at the sentencing hearing. Violence was deplorable, he told the judge, but South Africa had pushed the defendants into an impossible situation, 'to bow their heads and submit, or to resist by force'.[38] Indeed, three years earlier Paton himself had been forced to submit to the government and surrender his passport, preventing him from taking his anti-apartheid sentiments abroad.[39]

Several prominent black journalists had also bowed their heads. In 1963 Can Themba went into exile in Swaziland, exhausted by the prospect of trying to stay clear of the political fray in South Africa. 'I heard more and more politics: bitter, heady, virulent stuff,' he wrote. 'It expressed, in venomous terms, the wrath of a people who had come to the damn-it-all threshold.'[40] In the wake of Sharpeville and Rivonia, apartheid had permeated the country so thoroughly that, in Can's view, hardly 'one square inch' of the country remained undisrupted. Claustrophobic and bitter, he decided he had to get out.

Nat, too, was being pushed to the edge. Throughout the summer, he made enquiries about international journalism jobs and fellowships, including several with the US and British embassies.[41] In September 1963, an agent from the American publisher Simon & Schuster, with whom Nat had corresponded concerning writers for *The Classic*, suggested that he apply for the Nieman fellowship at Harvard, the same journalism scholarship that had taken Lewis Nkosi to the United States without a return ticket three years earlier.[42] In early 1964, Nat submitted an application to the programme. Backed by his impressive CV, which included 54 articles in

Nat's father, Chamberlain Nakasa, was a writer and typesetter in Durban, who had a regular column for the city's Zulu weekly, Ilanga lase Natal.

© *Courtesy Nakasa family*

Nat was only 20 years old when he moved to Johannesburg in late 1957 to take up a job at Drum *magazine.*

© Jürgen Schadeberg

The offices of Drum, *1954. Pictured here are many of the writers Nat read as a young man, including Henry Nxumalo (far left) and Can Themba (standing against wall, in the white shirt)*

In the early 1960s, Nat Nakasa stayed in this house in the Orlando West neighbourhood of Soweto, pressed up against the railway line that carried black workers to and from the city of Johannesburg each day.

```
TO:  NATHANIEL @ NATHAN NAKASE,
     8348 ORLANDO WEST,
     JOHANNESBURG.


     NOTICE IN TERMS OF PARAGRAPH (a) OF SUB-SECTION (1)
     OF SECTION TEN OF THE SUPPRESSION OF COMMUNISM ACT,
                 1950 (ACT NO. 44 OF 1950).


     WHEREAS I, BALTHAZAR JOHANNES VORSTER, Minister of
Justice of the Republic of South Africa, am satisfied
that you are engaged in activities which are furthering
or may further the achievement of the objects of communism,
I hereby, in terms of paragraph (a) of sub-section (1)
of section ten of the Suppression of Communism Act, 1950
```

Unsigned banning order for Nathaniel Nakasa (a slash has been drawn in pen across the document). Nat went into exile before the order could be signed.

UNITED STATES DEPARTMENT OF JUSTICE
FEDERAL BUREAU OF INVESTIGATION

In Reply, Please Refer to
File No.

Boston, Massachusetts.
April 28, 1965

ALL INFORMATION CONTAINED
HEREIN IS UNCLASSIFIED
DATE 10-25-2010 BY 60322 uc/lp/stp/fls

NATHANIEL NAKASA

On February 5, 1965, personnel, Immigration and Naturalization Service (INS), Boston, Massachusetts, advised that Nathaniel Nakasa had recently been interviewed by INS personnel concerning a possible extension of stay in the United States. Nakasa is identical with the subject of INS file A13-968-005. A review of this file on February 18, 1965 showed that Nathaniel Nakasa had been born May 12, 1937 at Durban, South Africa.

The opening page of the FBI file on Nathaniel Nakasa, which was declassified for the first time in 2010 at the request of the author.

The 1965 class of Nieman fellows at Harvard.

© Courtesy Nieman Foundation

Nat Nakasa's childhood home in the township of Chesterville, near Durban.

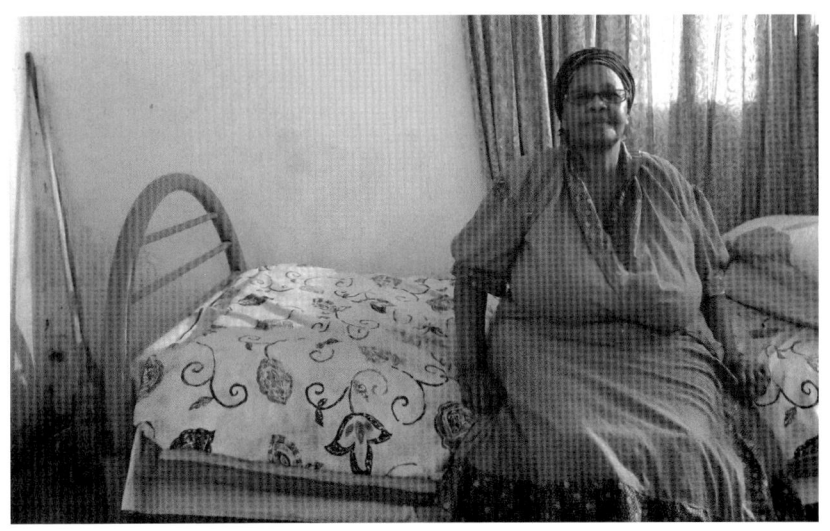

Nat Nakasa's only sister, Gladys Maphumulo, at her home outside Durban in August 2012.

© Courtesy Nakasa family

Nat's sister, Gladys, receives the Order of Ikhamanga on his behalf from President Thabo Mbeki. The award honours South Africans who have made outstanding contributions to the country's cultural life.

© Ryan Brown

Nat Nakasa is buried in Ferncliff Cemetery outside New York City. His grave was unmarked until the 1990s, when the Nieman Foundation at Harvard paid to have this marker installed.

Drum and an article in the *New York Times* magazine, Nat also got a recommendation letter from Nadine. She, in turn, asked her friend Helen Suzman – at that time the only MP who opposed apartheid outright – to write the second letter of support. Though Helen didn't know this friend of her daughter's particularly well, she agreed to help. 'It is his ambition to make a contribution to the development of literature on the African continent and I believe that his character and ability recommend him,' she wrote. 'It is rare indeed to find an African who has managed, despite all the difficulties, to throw off any racial resentments as has done Mr. Nakasa.'[43]

But even as he turned his sights beyond South Africa's borders, Nat's career in Johannesburg had also taken an unexpected turn. Around the same time as he put the finishing touches on his Nieman portfolio, he received a call from Allister Sparks, then the deputy editor of the *Rand Daily Mail*, one of the few anti-apartheid broadsheets still in publication. He had noticed Nat's work in *Drum*, he said, and wanted to know if the writer would be interested in running a column in his newspaper. He told Nat that the *Mail* felt it was time they had a black columnist, someone who could convey the African experience to their readership, and Nat's writing struck him as 'easy and articulate', a rare voice that could reach across racial lines. What was more, Allister insisted, Nat was 'damn near the only black voice of dissent' still publishing in the country, making him a provocative addition to the paper's editorial page.[44]

Nat wasted no time in accepting the *Mail*'s offer. In March

1964, he began trekking each Tuesday to the *Mail*'s office, where he and Allister would survey the 'fantastic range of ideas' he'd assembled for that week's column. 'The paper's black readership was growing rapidly but nonetheless most of the readers were white,' Allister said. 'So I told him I just wanted him to write about things that struck him in his everyday life as a very bright, smart young black guy.' So Nat came armed with observations and anecdotes, and together the two men whittled them down into a workable column subject. Then Nat would trudge home to begin work on his column for the Saturday edition of the paper.

The column at first made him quite nervous, and he would spend the days before it was due in a nervous frenzy. 'I've never known a journalist who worked that hard on a column,' said his friend Rose Phahle.[45] But that nervous energy didn't always translate into efficiency. Quite often, he said, Nat's Thursday deadline came and went without an inch of the thing written. And as Friday rolled around, late in the evening Nat would still be hunched over his typewriter, frantically trying to churn out something that would impress Allister and the other editors.

That autumn, the columns began to appear weekly in the paper beneath a small photograph and the pithy tagline 'As I See It'. From the outset, they were deeply personal, records of the moments when his own life came crashing up against National Party rule. Slotted amidst a sea of white faces on the editorial pages, the column offered an immediacy about the impacts of apartheid that appeared nowhere else in the paper. 'Nat's column was based on what was really happening,

A Native of Nowhere

the funny side of the township life and the absurdities of apartheid,' Rose said. He ventured only timidly into the folds of national politics, preferring instead to associate his name with the strange details of black life under apartheid.

These details took many forms. One week, he wrote of a harebrained labour 'crisis' whose only reason for existing was that the government refused to employ skilled black workers in many industries.[46] Another week he remarked on the strange fate of a university-educated African friend who worked in public relations but lost his job because the government refused to issue him with a passport to travel for business. 'I keep telling him he should never have allowed himself to become so highly educated,' Nat wrote. 'Without all those degrees he could slip quietly into a pass office job and have himself a ball stamping reference books.'[47] A third piece painted Johannesburg as a city with a split face, where non-whites felt like 'someone who has unwittingly volunteered to become the guinea pig in some incredible experiment by a quack scientist'.[48]

Sarcastic, clever and sometimes painfully self-aware, Nat's columns marched his white readers into the South Africa of the majority. One week, he travelled to the Transkei, a newly created 'homeland' for Xhosa people in the southeastern part of the country, to report on the opening of the new country's Parliament. That year, the National Party had declared the region a self-governing territory, to be managed by African rulers with strong ties to the white government in Pretoria. It was a sham institution, and Nat didn't have to wait long to see why. When he pulled up at the building, he immediately spied

111

two of the MPs sitting on the kerb, chatting their way through a lunch of a loaf of bread and a bottle of Coke – the classic lunch of a Johannesburg labourer. 'Not really befitting of a chief,' Nat whispered to Rose, who was travelling with him. That night, they visited the MPs' 'hotel', a squalid dormitory with rats scraping around beneath broken floorboards. The so-called leadership of the new homeland slept in a single room, on old cots. Nat was flabbergasted. 'Do you think in the other parliament, the one in Cape Town, they live like this?' he asked them. But when he returned to Johannesburg to write up the piece, he had to admit that, despite the obvious farce of the new homeland, he hadn't been able to let go fully of the excitement of getting to cover a national legislature for the first time. After all, covering the South African Parliament was 'something for whites only'. As a result, 'even going to the Transkeian Legislative Assembly ... was bound to be a major personal experience for me'.[49]

Nat also used his column to take aim at his critics. During his years in Johannesburg, Nat's position as a 'darling of the white activist community' had only solidified, and working for a white newspaper certainly didn't help his case.[50] His column for the *Rand Daily Mail* became an act of defiance, challenging not only apartheid but the increasing polarisation of black politics. 'People who want me to adopt their ideas simply must first earn my respect,' he wrote. 'That applies to African nationalists who may threaten to do me in if I say or write that [President of Ghana Kwame] Nkrumah is now a dictator. It also applies to people who make laws, backed by force and not majority will.'[51] Nat had never been at home ideologically with either the government or the black resistance movement, but in the *Rand Daily Mail* he had at last found a written outlet for that frustration, and an audience that also understood, perhaps even more than he did, what it was like to stand astride those worlds.

In April 1964, Harvard called. Nat had been invited to join the 1965 class of Nieman fellows. His selection brought him together with a world-class assemblage of young journalists. The other men awarded the Nieman that year included Ray Jenkins, the civil rights beat reporter for the *Montgomery Advertiser*, Smith Hempstone, a fiery *LA Times* columnist who would go on to serve as US Ambassador to Kenya, and Shankar Sarda, a journalist from India who had served as editor of four newspapers.[52]

But for Nat, the good news ended there. Like Lewis before him, he was soon engaged in a protracted battle with the state for permission to travel, a permission he was determined to obtain. 'Heaven knows the last thing I want is an exit permit,' he wrote. In June he perhaps naively reassured the Nieman Foundation, 'as I have never been active in politics except as a journalist, I expect no difficulty in obtaining a passport'.[53] That confidence was soon deflated when, months after his application went in, he was still without travel documents.

In the three years since Lewis accepted an exit permit and travelled to the United States as a stateless man, the government had become increasingly alert to how it could use the issue of emigration to its own political gain. Dissident elites, they realised, could be frustrated into submission by the seemingly arbitrary refusal of travel documents or, as in the case of Lewis, by being allowed to leave only on the condition of permanently forfeiting their citizenship. Between 1962 and 1964, the state refused some 647 passport applications, all without ever developing a coherent policy on who could not leave, or why. Passport control rested entirely at the opaque level of bureaucracy, where it was nearly impossible to trace or unravel.[54] In this manner, Nat's application joined hundreds of others that disappeared into the black hole of the system.

Frequently existing on the cusp of political activism, artists and intellectuals faced a particularly high level of uncertainty. In the years preceding Nat's passport application, he had watched as the *Drum* writers Es'kia Mphahlele and Todd Matshikiza were granted passports, while Bloke Modisane and Lewis Nkosi were denied them. The musicians Miriam Makeba and Hugh Masekela, to whom Nat would be close in the United States, had managed to secure passports, but Hugh's sister Barbara was forced to leave on an exit permit.[55]

Nat still had no idea what would become of his application when, one morning, he awoke at his house in Orlando to a pounding on the door. When he answered it, Rose was standing there. Listen, his friend told him, he'd been raided by the police and was now on his way to the station to work it out. He said the police had come to his room in the middle of the night and began turning the place over, searching for something that would tie him to a group of activists in Cape Town awaiting charges for anti-apartheid organising. They pulled books off the shelves and searched beneath his mattress. When they couldn't find anything in his room, they began going through his car. There, in the glovebox, they found a note he'd written to friends in the UK asking them to help raise money for the trial of the activists. The police told him to get dressed, that he was under arrest. But as soon as he was ready to go, they suddenly changed their mind and told him to report to the police station first thing in the morning.

So, he explained to Nat, that's where he was headed. He thought he'd be fine, he said. After all, if they had really wanted to arrest him, wouldn't they have just taken him in the night before? But he'd had enough experience with South African police in the past to know that whenever you stepped into a police station, for whatever reason, you had better tell someone where you were. Otherwise, if you went missing it could be days before anyone realised it. If Rose wasn't back in a few hours, he asked, could Nat go to the station to see what had happened? Nat gave his assent and his friend headed off.

A half-hour passed, then another. Rose still hadn't circled back to Nat's place to let him know he was all right, so Nat decided to walk over to the station himself. 'It was a very brave thing to do,' Rose said. 'None of us walked into that station unless we were summoned.' Inside, Nat approached the front desk and asked what had happened to his friend. The sergeant behind the desk laughed. 'He's gone,' he said. 'We sent him home.' Then he looked squarely at Nat. 'But I know who you are too,' he said. 'You're Nat Nakasa. You think we're going to give you a passport? Never.'[56] Then he walked off.

Sure enough, in September, the month the Nieman fellowship officially began in Cambridge, Massachusetts, he received word that his application had been denied. 'It is a matter of grave concern', wrote the Bantu Affairs Commissioner of the Witwatersrand in an internal memo concerning his application, 'that his [writing] should stimulate disaffection and unrest among the Bantu population.'[57] Although Nat himself was never privy to that correspondence, the reality was clear: if he wanted to go, he would have to leave on an exit permit, without the option of return. 'I hate apartheid,' Nat wrote to Thompson, 'but this is my home, this is where I want to live … not as an exile.'[58] The choice was a chilling one – continue the life he had managed to carve out under the apartheid state, with a successful career and a rising new magazine, or, as Nadine put it, 'accept exile as the price of a breath of the open world'.[59]

As he weighed these options, Nat took note of the empty seats in the *Drum* office and his favourite bars. Many of those who had been mentors, friends and colleagues of the young writer from the time he stepped off the train from Durban were already gone from Johannesburg. With leading African intellectuals increasingly silenced by banning orders that prohibited them from publishing or organising and powerful political activists like Mandela and Walter Sisulu imprisoned for life on Robben Island, surviving as a black writer in South Africa had begun to feel for many of Nat's friends like a losing battle. Just within the previous year, Can and another prominent fiction writer and *Drum* contributor, Bessie Head, had chosen exile rather than remaining under the apartheid state. For Nat, too, the gallivanting antics of 'fringe country' had lost their appeal. 'The business of expecting war each time I go to buy a stamp has ceased to be a game,' he remarked sadly in a column for the *Rand Daily Mail*. 'There are too many moments when I feel like giving in and letting this country go the way of its choice.'[60]

By this time, Nat also had a serious girlfriend, a teacher named Sheila, which might have been a reason to stay, if she herself weren't also preparing to leave. Around the time that Nat received word that he'd won the Nieman, Sheila learned that she had been awarded a Fulbright fellowship to study at Ball State University in Indiana. But unlike Nat, she'd had little trouble acquiring a passport. And with good reason. Her father, a school principal in the Orange Free State town of Kroonstad, had been an inspector for the Bantu Education Department. Her application slid easily through the system. She received a passport in less than a month.[61]

Meanwhile, the South Africa Nat knew was also quite literally disintegrating around him. Transkei, the Xhosa homeland he had recently visited for a *Mail* column, was only the first piece of a larger National Party project to splinter the African population into discrete, autonomous 'tribes', each linked to a particular strip of desolate, undeveloped land that was their supposed territorial homeland. Although the stated aim of the project was to grant new autonomy to African peoples, in fact the carving up of the country marked a shift by the government toward a more complete version of apartheid, one in which blacks would cease even to be South Africans at all.

At the very moment that Nat found himself on the brink of giving up his own citizenship, some three and a half million of his countrymen, or 10 per cent of the total population, faced a similar fate, forced to renounce their homes and South African identity to join their 'tribe' on its purported ancestral land.[62] Although Nat's choice to leave the country came about through markedly different circumstances from those of the victims of forced removals, both parties shared an essential common thread – they had the rotten luck to be standing in the way when their country decided to purge itself of its own people.

Whether or not Nat knew it, he had also drawn the probing gaze of the South African police, and if he stayed in South Africa, his time as a free man was about to come to an unceremonious end. An extensive file on the writer kept by the Department of Justice shows that the police had been tailing him since May 1959, when he was first observed 'attending a coloured party at Heidelberg apartment 19, Pretoria'.[63] Over the next five years, police records indicate that Nat was followed on at least 26 separate occasions, to ANC meetings and mixed-race parties, to secret gatherings with 'likely communists' and *Drum* interviews with 'well known left-leaning person[s]'. 'He is known everywhere as an enemy of the ruling government,' the police report explained, 'in particular with the Afrikaans general public.' The police further intercepted his correspondence and kept a file of his writing, quoting both extensively in defence of their assertion that Nat constituted a major danger to the state. 'The promotion of animosity between whites and non-whites is one of ... the marks of communism in South Africa,' the file noted. 'Through his communication and declarations [Nat Nakasa] advances [these] aims.' Thus, under the notorious Suppression of Communism Act, the Justice Secretary ordered that Nat be banned for a period of five years, concluding in September 1969.[64]

The command, however, would never be issued. Nat had already decided to accept the exit permit, forgoing any possibility that he might return to South Africa. Tucked into the pages of his police surveillance file is an unsigned copy of his banning order, awaiting the final approval of the Minister of Justice (and future Prime Minister), B.J. Vorster.[65] By all accounts, his escape came just in time.

But that did not mean the choice was easy. Deflated, he wrote to Jack Thompson in July, 'I just can't get used to the power of these men and what they can do with it. I wish someone could explain to them ... that giving me a passport and letting me go to school for the first time in my life cannot do any harm to this country or apartheid for that matter.'[66] In a parting column for the *Rand Daily Mail* entitled 'A Native of Nowhere', he explained the uneasiness of forfeiting his citizenship. 'Once out I shall apparently become a stateless person, a wanderer.'[67] Without citizenship in any nation, he wouldn't even be able to enter the United States. He first had to find a country that would issue him with a passport, or else persuade the Americans to waive their most basic requirement for entry. Any way he approached it, travelling without a passport would be an arduous task.

For those acquaintances who remained in South Africa, Nat's choice to leave came not as a shock, but rather a sad inevitability. One reader of the *Rand Daily Mail* wrote to the editor that he or she was 'distressed but not surprised' by Nat's choice to go, calling his columns 'quite a revelation' for many of the paper's readers.[68] 'By that time so many of our friends were in and out of detention, hounded down by the police,' Nadine Gordimer remembered. 'So we all thought yes, he's young, he should leave while it's possible.'[69] Apartheid would eventually end, Nadine reasoned, and in the meantime, Nat had the chance of an education, a view of the world beyond South Africa's borders.

Still, in the final days before his flight was to leave, Nat balked. He frantically began calling friends, pleading for them to tell him if he was making the right decision. 'He just didn't want to go,' said David Hazelhurst, former editor of *Drum*. Over drinks, Nat told him that with the government hunkering down, he worried that leaving might be permanent. David pushed back: it could be a long time before you come back, he said, but it will be worth it. But Nat was unconvinced. The night before he was set to leave, he phoned Allister Sparks and told him he needed to talk. When he arrived at Allister's place in Norwood, 'he was agonising'.

'I can't do this,' he told his friend. Long into the night they argued it over. Allister pointed to the example of Lewis, who by then was living in England and working for the BBC. Abroad, he told his young charge, Nat could grow as a writer without the burden of apartheid hanging over him all the time. 'The system here can't last forever,' he said. 'You'll be able to come back, and when you do, you'll be a major figure.' Tentatively, Nat agreed, and the two men parted. For decades, Allister said, that night haunted him. 'I pushed him into doing it,' he remarked. 'I've [always] had a huge sense of guilt about what happened to him.'[70]

But Nat had made his choice. Two days later, after missing his first flight, he was accompanied by Nadine and several other friends to Jan Smuts International Airport in Johannesburg to travel to Lusaka, Northern Rhodesia (which would become Zambia the following month), where he hoped to gain a more internationally recognised travel document in order to enter the United States.[71] As the group milled about in the terminal, Alf Kumalo snapped a series of photographs. In them, Nat was dressed smartly in a full suit with a skinny black tie. He looks serious, nervous perhaps. His smile is strained. Nadine, her hair done up in a tall beehive, stares at him sombrely.

At the passport control counter, he laid out his flimsy exit permit, which spelled out the specifics of his departure in no uncertain terms: if he ever returned to the country of his birth, he would be arrested. Printed across the bottom of the page in large block lettering was the phrase 'This is a valuable document. Keep it in a safe place.'[72] The clerk behind the counter stamped it and, with that, Nat was gone – from Cato Manor and Sophiatown and Soweto, from the chaotic *Drum* office and the pages of the *Rand Daily Mail*, from the shebeens and the coffee bars owned by wayward Texans. As he stepped onto the plane that day, he, like many South African artists and intellectuals before and after him, slipped out of the only world he had ever known, and stepped into a new and uncertain life. 'What this means', he explained to his *Mail* readers, 'is that self-confessed Europeans are in a position to declare me, an African, a prohibited immigrant on African soil. Nothing intrigues me more.'[73]

The moment Nat boarded his flight that day in 1964, he entered a dark rift. By law, he was no longer a South African, but by blood and personal history he was rooted only there. In giving up his citizenship, he had stepped out of the legal binds of being an African under apartheid. What he had traded them for, however, was the precarious uncertainty of the refugee, wholly at the will of the international community to give him a place to set down his bags. Indeed, his position was so fragile, so fraught and dangerous, that it is nearly impossible to imagine why he would have accepted it unless he truly felt he had no other choice.

In a sense, that was true. Although in 1961 Nat had been able to take Lewis's departure in his stride, by 1964 nearly every major black writer in South Africa had been banned, along with a number of liberal white writers. The bulk of the anti-apartheid movement's leadership was in prison, exile or underground. Even if he didn't know the extent or content of the government's surveillance on him, Nat certainly knew from the experiences of those around him that the National Party kept tabs on those it feared, and that it had the capacity to lash out with great success at anyone who frustrated its vision of a segregated, hierarchical South Africa. In this climate, the 'fringe country' culture that had once been the source of so much possibility in Nat's life now stood in his way. He had risen as far as he could within its confines; beyond it, South Africa was a solid brick wall for a talented and ambitious African writer.

Indeed, all the government had to do was label someone a communist, and instantly he or she was an illegal presence. In the unique shorthand of the apartheid state, 'communist' stood in for dissident, activist, intellectual and protester, offering an internationally comprehensible way for the South African government to mark its enemies. The United States spoke this language as well, although if Nat is any indication, some nuances occasionally got lost in translation. Despite the fact that the two countries professed a shared desire to defeat communism wherever it lurked, including within the anti-apartheid movement, Nat's experience suggests that they never entirely agreed on a definition of exactly what they were fighting. As the South African justice system moved to stamp Nat as a communist for writing and living a critique of apartheid, the CIA propped up those very same activities in order to cultivate the young writer's potential to steer his politically charged country clear of communist influence. Both countries deliberately used the globalised term to lend international political weight to how they approached Nat, but for each the word 'communist' obscured a particular and localised meaning and purpose.

Of course, Nat himself was unaware of the entire conflict, as none of its actors had considered including him in their discussion of his ideological leanings. Instead, as he prepared to leave South Africa, he likely had other, more practical concerns. Even in a highly repressive society, exile was not a decision to be made lightly. It meant not only accepting that he might never return, but also taking on the isolation of being a South African in the United States. Although many of his colleagues and friends preceded him into exile, they had chosen to leave in the same chaotic, individualistic way they had always lived in South Africa, scattering themselves across the globe. Lewis Nkosi and Bloke Modisane went to England, Can Themba to Swaziland, Bessie Head to Botswana, Es'kia Mphahlele to France, and Todd Matshikiza to Northern Rhodesia.[74] Although all of them remained writers and vocal critics of apartheid, the closeness and sense of urgency that had characterised their community within South Africa faded. As Bloke wrote, 'Everything I had known, loved, and hated remained behind me ... But ... the problem was still with me; only its immediacy was removed.'[75] Watching from afar as apartheid continued to bear down on their country, many of these writers found themselves for the first time profoundly alone.

In March 1963, a year and a half before Nat left South Africa, his fellow *Drum* writer Casey Motsisi wrote a piece for the magazine in tribute to the dozens of artists and intellectuals who had already left the country. As the article rattled off a list of prominent black South Africans in exile, it provided both a portrait of the decimated community Nat was leaving and a sense of the profound nostalgia of those who stayed behind. 'Life gets pretty dull around the old burg sometimes now ...

without the goings on and the gossip and gaiety you gave it,' Motsisi wrote sadly. 'I just hope those characters in London and the U.S.A. appreciate what they've got, that's all.'[76]

Six

THEY WOULD HAVE MADE a curious pair on the streets of Dar es Salaam, Tanganyika: the slight young journalist with the crisp, rolling accent of the missionary-educated South African, and the American ten years his senior and nearly a foot taller, dressed in a suit and his trademark black-rimmed glasses. But while Nat and Malcolm X may have carried themselves rather differently, 'he was an American Negro in East Africa: I was a journalist from Johannesburg,' Nat later told a reporter matter-of-factly, so naturally 'there were lots of things to talk about'. The day they met, Malcolm X enthusiastically explained to Nat his belief in pan-Africanism, a breathless take on black pride that swept across borders and oceans and struck a chord with the young South African writer. 'A lot of the things he said were things [we Africans] wanted to have said, but lacked the equipment,' Nat later recalled.

The two had met in the lobby of a Dar hotel. Malcolm was in the city as part of a whirlwind tour across the continent designed to establish connections between the newly

A Native of Nowhere

independent nations of Africa and black Americans. Nat was there restlessly awaiting permission to enter the United States. By then, Malcolm X was already an international figure, known widely as the black nationalist who had pushed questions of African American rights in a more militant and radical direction. But by 1964, he had shifted his focus from advocating black separatism to attempting to establish an internationally based black movement for human rights. As Nat remembered it, the newly remade leader was 'a very warm personality who's had a raw deal'.[1] That was a familiar feeling to the newly stateless Nat, and it didn't take long for the two men to hit it off.

Within days, however, Malcolm was gone, jetting off to the next point on his nine-country African tour. But Nat stayed behind, and the encounter left him reeling. As his friend Hugh Masekela later remembered it, he would spend a great deal of time in the year to come mulling over their political discussions.[2] The American leader's insistence on quickening the pace of change in the civil rights movement resonated with the South African, perhaps for no other reason than the raw and recent memory of how he had been betrayed by his own country. Malcolm also presented a far more bitter perspective about black life in the United States than Nat had likely come across in South Africa, where the American civil rights movement had been presented to him as a noble and largely successful struggle.[3] 'He was in shock at what he heard,' Hugh remembered.[4]

However, as his discussions with Malcolm rattled around in his head, Nat also had a much more immediate concern. He was stuck. He had left South Africa with only his exit permit, and he still needed a passport or visa to enter the United States. In Cambridge, Massachusetts, his fellowship was sliding by, and he no longer had a way back to the country he had left. His time as a 'native of nowhere' had officially begun.

As he waited in Lusaka for his diplomatic permissions to come through, he spent the week with Todd Matshikiza, an older *Drum* colleague, and his wife, Esmé. The two had left South Africa for London four years earlier and had recently moved to Lusaka so that Todd could take up a job with the fledgling Zambia Broadcasting Corporation. When Nat came to visit, Esmé said, the mood was optimistic. 'We still hoped then that we'd be able to get back home,' she said. This moment, this lifestyle, these three South Africans gathered in a little house in Zambia, were all transitory. None of them felt weighed down by their circumstance, she said, because none of them thought they would be staying.[5]

After a few days with the Matshikizas, on 24 September, Nat received word from the State Department in Washington that he must proceed to another 'friendly country' and apply for a passport or travel permit there. Only then would he be granted permission to enter the United States.[6] Begrudgingly, he signed an application for a visa at the consulate in Lusaka and proceeded to Dar es Salaam in pursuit of a travel document less flimsy than a South African exit permit.[7] 'For the time being,' Nat wrote to his *Rand Daily Mail* readers from abroad, 'my future lies in a number of diplomatic bags.'[8]

As a black South African in Dar, Nat found himself marvelling at the basic way the country functioned. Blacks ran the shops and the law offices, directed traffic, took your ticket at the airport. They were the patrons and the owners in its fancy hotels, its restaurants, its swanky bars. After more than two decades in South Africa, this was a remarkable thing to witness – the basic mechanics of a country that didn't have to devote the bulk of its national energy to the project of segregation.

But it wasn't where he wanted to be. After his meeting with Malcolm X, Nat continued circling the city, waiting on the US government to decide if he'd be allowed to enter the country. It was nearly the end of October before the State Department finally cut him loose. All he had to do now was fly on to London to process his passport waiver.[9] But as Nat waited in the British capital, he confessed to his *Rand Daily Mail* readers that parading himself before an endless stream of immigration officials to explain the painful fact that he had no country had begun to wear him down. It 'drained the last bit of energy out of me,' he wrote.[10] And even though the permission to travel to the United States had come at last, it was highly provisional. As he boarded the plane to New York City, he carried a visa granting him permission to be in the United States for only five months, until 10 March 1965.[11]

Still, the excitement of travelling to the United States was enough to keep him going, at least for the moment. Scrunched into his seat on the KLM flight across the Atlantic, an old man sitting behind Nat struck up a conversation. 'Say,' the man asked, 'who won the World Series?' He hadn't even entered American airspace yet, Nat realised, but he had already been mistaken for an 'American negro'. 'I had no idea what [the World Series] was,' he admitted later, 'but we had a friendly conversation nonetheless.' Americans, he reported in the *Mail* a few weeks later, were a 'gay, friendly lot', a welcoming crowd for a young man thousands of miles from home.[12]

When his flight touched down, however, he saw to his dismay that New York City looked like 'a great, modern slum', a mass of red brick buildings with the eerie look of 'filing cabinets with people packed neatly inside'. The gloomy pallor of Manhattan caught him off-guard, but the city also offered something unexpectedly hopeful. On his first day in the United States, he attended a concert by the South African jazz musician and fellow exile Hugh Masekela in Greenwich Village. Over the skittering notes of Hugh's trumpet, Nat talked with his wife, the immensely popular South African singer, Miriam Makeba, and her daughter about their lives in exile. When the girl declared to him that she wanted to become a lawyer, Nat realised to his surprise that in this country 'there was nothing to stop her'.[13]

Seven

SOMETIME AFTER NAT ARRIVED at Harvard in October 1964, a photographer snapped an official portrait of his class of Nieman fellows. In the image, he stands in the front row, his tweed jacket buttoned over a thin striped tie. The only black man in the group, he is also the youngest. Surrounded by balding heads and Buddy Holly glasses, he holds his hands behind his back and flashes the camera a thin-lipped smile. The stiff, professional image is a kind of photographic mirror for Nat's own vision of Harvard, as an insular place 'steeped in the sombre business of education'.[1] Only months before the photo was taken, he had been crafting slyly mocking critiques of apartheid for the *Rand Daily Mail* and sneaking across Johannesburg to attend multiracial parties. Now, the bustle and sharp edges of that world had given way to a measured life of college seminars and invitations to speak about the 'African experience of apartheid' for audiences of curious Americans. A young African man who had spent his life ducking and jabbing at the apartheid state, Nat found himself for the first time trying to manoeuvre through a world where racial politics often appeared to be just another subject of academic discourse, solemn and removed.

In South Africa, Nat had always lived by what he opposed: the rule of a white minority over a black majority. But in the United States, where the president had a civil rights agenda but police jailed African American activists for peaceful protest, where black nationalists drew crowds but so did segregationist senators, the complex racial landscape was foreign and often impenetrable to an outsider. Although in South Africa Nat had never been party to the organised opposition movement, his life carried an urgency and moral clarity that he found he could not recreate in the United States. The rigidity of apartheid meant that if nothing else, Nat and his circle of friends knew what side they were on. As Allister Sparks put it, 'the cowboys and the crooks are easy to find and you can map your own moral path through all of that quite easily.' But life without Sophiatown or Sharpeville, Nat discovered, did not cure him of his sharp sense of the world's injustice. It simply left him without someone to address that anger to, adrift in a country whose inequalities made little sense to him.

Eight thousand miles from the 'fringe country' world that breathed life into his journalism career, in the United States Nat existed on the fringe in an entirely different way. The community of wise-cracking South African intellectuals with whom he had come of age was gone, replaced by American professors, students and writers with whom he struggled to connect. The few South Africans he knew in the United States lived in other cities, unable to help him manage the lonely experience of exile on a day-to-day level. Even more jarringly, Nat knew that, whatever the connections he made in the United States, he would not be able to stay there. The Immigration and Naturalization Services (INS) had granted him an extension of his initial visa – from 10 March 1965 to 31 August – but it was still only a one-year student visa, and it was not renewable.[2] Without either permanent residency or a community of South Africans in exile to be part of, Nat could only skim across the surface of American life, never able to put down roots or develop a coherent sense of purpose in his new country.

Indeed, in the ten months he spent in the United States, Nat published only two pieces of writing – a final column for the *Rand Daily Mail* and an essay for the *New York Times* – and appears to have made no close friends. As a result, decades later the last year of his life reveals itself only in fragments – some of them contradictory, all of them incomplete. Characters float in and out of the narrative, speaking vaguely of a 'shy and reticent' man with whom they occasionally ate lunch, talked or attended class.[3] When asked in 2010 about Nat's mental state near the end of his life, his friend and fellow South African exile Hugh Masekela shook his head and said he hadn't known him that way.[4] In fact, it seems no one had – the most systematic and detailed record of his time in the United States is the surveillance file kept by the Federal Bureau of Investigation (FBI) to monitor his immigration status. But whatever gaps these materials leave, they cannot be counterbalanced with information provided by Nat himself, for although others allude to his personal belongings, letters and unpublished writing in the United States, none of these materials survived his death.

However, these holes in the historical record are themselves telling. They reveal a life lived in soft focus, held at a distance from the people and experiences around it. In doing so, the gaps speak indirectly to how exile could have undone a talented writer like Nat at what should have been the apex of his career. 'I cannot laugh anymore,' he is said to have told a friend in the United States, 'and when I cannot laugh, I cannot write.'[5] Exile stripped Nat not only of South Africa, but also of his own centre of gravity. Without *Drum*, without Johannesburg, without apartheid to push back against, he became unmoored in the United States, disconnected even from his previous self. As Es'kia Mphahlele, a fellow writer for *Drum* and *The Classic*, wrote of his own experience in exile, 'you seem more than ever before to be monitoring every response you are making to what happens to you ... as if you were contemplating a personality moving in front of your eyes. As if it wouldn't surprise you to have to monitor your own funeral.'[6]

Writing of his experiences leaving Nigeria for London, the writer Chinua Achebe noted that Westerners 'roamed the world with the confidence of the authority of their homeland behind them'. But 'the experience of a traveller from the world's poor places is very different,' he continued. 'Let me just say of such a traveller that he will not be able to claim a double citizenship like Gertrude Stein when she said: "I am an American and Paris is my hometown."'[7] Indeed, at the moment Nat arrived at Harvard, for all the government was concerned, he was not a South African anymore, and Boston certainly wasn't his hometown.

The experience was, at first, exciting. Loosely structured, the Nieman fellowship programme offered approximately fifteen talented mid-career journalists from around the world a year of broad access to the elite university's resources and each other. The 1965 class that awaited Nat included newsmen from eight different countries, including India, Iran and South Korea, and reporters for the *New York Times*, the *Boston Globe* and the *Los Angeles Times*.[8] Each Tuesday, the contingent of writers gathered at the Nieman office for a seminar with a Harvard professor, and each Thursday the programme held a weekly Nieman dinner.[9]

Aside from those two engagements, the fellows were free to do what they wished to engage in the intellectual life of the university – take classes, join organisations, give talks. But perhaps most staggering for a black man stepping out of apartheid South Africa, they simply came and went as they pleased on campus: strolling through Harvard Yard, eating in campus dining halls, and scanning the stacks in the massive Widener Library. There was no curfew and no one to ask for your pass, no authorities to be duped or shebeens to sneak into, no need to worry that the next article you wrote could have you silenced by the government. 'There aren't any policemen around asking you questions, and there aren't any restrictions,' Nat told a reporter for the *Harvard Crimson*, the student newspaper.[10] For the first time in his life, he didn't have to break the law just to get by.

But although the university would have seemed almost absurdly open to someone like Nat, for many of its students Harvard was exactly the opposite – stuffy and in certain regards a bit outdated. As student protests erupted at universities across the country in the mid-1960s to challenge US foreign policy, domestic inequality and the intellectual rigidity of universities, Harvard men still followed the tradition of taking their meals in the school's dining halls wearing a jacket and tie. 'Our expectation is you will behave like gentlemen,' the dean of the college, John Monro, told the entering class of freshmen in 1965.[11] And though women took virtually all of their classes with Harvard's gentlemen, they still technically attended their own separate, single-sex college, Radcliffe. And black students were a tiny minority of the student populations.[12] Indeed, even the simple creation of a black student group had been hotly contested, and did not come to fruition until the spring of 1963.[13] By the end of 1964, student activism was slowly rising in profile, but it remained stymied by a long and deeply conservative institutional history.

When Nat arrived at Harvard, however, he found himself unwittingly placed at the centre of that budding student protest movement. The youngest Nieman fellow in the class of 1965 and its only unmarried member, he was put up in Adams House, one of the college's nine residential communities for undergraduates. A cluster of smart red brick buildings near Harvard Square, the house was known for the distinctly bohemian bent of its students, and by 1964 had become a nexus for political activity on campus. The house hosted meetings for several progressive campus groups, including Harvard's branch of the newly formed Students for a Democratic Society (SDS), a national student protest group founded in Ann Arbor, Michigan, two years earlier. Many of the organisation's members lived in Adams, exchanging banter about civil rights, student activism and American politics over meals in the house's ornate, wood-panelled dining hall.[14]

Although Nat was several years older than these undergraduates, he fell in more easily with them than with the other Nieman fellows. While the rest of the men in the programme had come to Harvard with their families, Nat, much like a student, had arrived alone. Fellow Nieman Ray Jenkins said that the South African stood at a distance from the rest of the group because he was younger and less settled.[15] Like the undergraduates Nat encountered, he had never been to university before, and his young-looking face belied his nearly decade-long career as a journalist, allowing him to slip easily into their social network. 'He looked quite like any other young Negro student on the yard,' Ray remembered.[16]

Early in the term, Nat befriended a black student and fellow Adams resident named Harold McDougall, who quickly became the young writer's sounding board for his early frustrations with Harvard life. Like many of the students around him – in fact, perhaps in part because of them – Nat's first few weeks in Cambridge had led him to see Harvard as rigidly and obtusely academic in its approach to questions of social change. At home in South Africa, he explained to Harold, discussions of race had been visceral, lived out on the

137

same streets where they took place. But at Harvard, students and professors seemed to approach blackness as merely another field to be studied, another academic concept to be defined and written about. And black students on campus, he was convinced, had bought into the complacency, determined to conduct themselves in a way that brought little attention to their race.[17]

But even more than being frustrated by the lack of engagement around issues of race at Harvard, he struggled to make sense of the very parameters of the debate. 'I could probably spend a year here without ever knowing the full meaning of being black in the United States,' he wrote soon after his arrival in Cambridge.[18] Although it was the American south that had received international attention for its civil rights movement in the late 1950s and early 1960s, northern cities like Boston were also on the boil. And like Johannesburg, Boston was a city parcelled. At the time Nat arrived, tensions were rising in the city over the vastly uneven quality of its public schools – divided not formally by law as in the southern states, but by the well-worn grooves of decades of residential segregation.

Part of the issue was that, like Johannesburg in the 1940s and 1950s, the city's skin tone was rapidly darkening. As black migrants from the American south came in search of jobs in the 1940s and 1950s, whites began to depart the inner city for the suburbs. Between 1940 and 1970, Boston's black population grew 342 per cent, to 104,000. Meanwhile, 31 per cent of the city's white occupants moved out. The resulting demographic shift meant that blacks rose from being 3 per cent of the city's population to making up 16 per cent at the time Nat arrived.[19] And the city's large working-class white community was beginning to feel the sting.

But as Nat quickly discovered, merely being black did not grant him special access to the content of the African American experience in Boston. To live as a black American was entirely different from living as a black South African, and the experiences defied simple comparisons. As Es'kia Mphahlele wrote of his own exile in the United States, 'I could only identify intellectually and emotionally with the black American's condition, but could not in any tangible, particular way feel his history.' Nat, too, experienced the phenomenon of wanting to identify but lacking the cultural capital. As Harold remembered, his friend frequently tried to greet black students he didn't know on campus. But while he saw this as a gesture of solidarity and perhaps the spark of a friendship, they were mortified that he would single them out for friendliness on nothing more than the colour of their skin. Blackness may have hopped oceans and cut across borders, but how it was experienced depended very much on where you stood.[20]

Aside from meeting Harold, Nat largely faded from view in the weeks after his arrival in Cambridge. Sources tell snippets of his opening months in the United States: he enrolled in courses in the Social Structure of Modern Africa and Negro History.[21] He asked a vivacious Radcliffe student on a date.[22]

He went to lunch once or twice at Harvard's faculty club with Ray Jenkins, fellow Nieman and the civil rights beat reporter for the *Montgomery Advertiser*.[23] But gone are the traces of his emotional reactions to this well-ordered life, the indications of how and when it began to dip. The next time someone took note of Nat's actions, however, his early frustrations with American race relations had multiplied, suggesting that the concerns he expressed to Harold were not just passing worries, but expressions of a wider isolation and confusion that were beginning to colour his world.

According to Ray, one afternoon in November or December the Nieman programme invited an assistant social psychology professor named Thomas Pettigrew to speak at the weekly seminar. Young and energetic, Professor Pettigrew was an expert on American race relations who had travelled widely – including to Nat's hometown of Durban – to conduct research on racial discrimination. He had a reputation for enjoying a few stiff drinks, and on these terms had become friendly with many of the Niemans, including, some have suggested, Nat.[24] That afternoon, however, the South African did not show up for the seminar, and so the speaker and the others began without him.

Then, midway through the discussion, Nat burst through the doors. Before he even sat down, Ray could smell the beer on his breath. Tom paused and then continued his talk. But Nat quickly interrupted him, challenging a small point he had made, a move 'quite within bounds for our robust Nieman seminars', Ray remembered.[25] Then suddenly, the young writer snapped. He began to berate Tom, rambling about drinking blood and judging civilisation, that the white man could never truly understand the position of the black man.[26] His speech was slurred and incoherent, a bumbling, apocalyptic narrative that Pettigrew said was 'nine-tenths incomprehensible'.[27] When Nat finished, he turned and left, leaving Tom and the shocked crowd of Niemans behind him.

When friends confronted him the next day about what he'd done, Nat was filled with embarrassment. He quickly approached those who had been at the seminar and made a brisk round of apologies. Tom remembered that Nat appeared 'chagrined' about what had happened. But for Ray, the outburst in some ways came as little surprise. Before it happened, he and the other Niemans had whispered that it was strange to see a black South African muster up so much coolness and detachment when he spoke about the calculating system of racial hierarchy under which he had grown up.[28] Now they realised it had only been a front. The pain had been sparking inside him all along, simply waiting for a way to explode outward.

After the incident with Tom Pettigrew, Nat began to withdraw from the other Niemans. He still came to seminars, but he was subdued and unresponsive. When other fellows invited him to informal social events in their homes, he rarely came – and, when he did, rarely spoke. Ray remembered that he would hover around the edges of a conversation, listening solemnly and occasionally inserting some pointed remark. And at

Harvard, he all but stopped attending the class the two men had together on the history of the American south.[29]

As Nat grew disillusioned with his life at Harvard, he began to grasp for an understanding of America beyond the ivory tower. Near the end of the term, he received another reporting assignment from the *New York Times*, this time to write a personal essay about his impressions of Harlem. Like his earlier piece on black life under apartheid, it was meant to be a reported collection of his impressions and encounters. But on a personal level, the assignment appeared at least partly driven by homesickness. 'I had visions of private homes turned into shebeens,' he wrote. 'Here I would find the drinking fraternity and be welcomed like a long-missed cousin.'[30] Perhaps, he thought, the black community that had eluded him at Harvard would emerge again in upper Manhattan.

But Harlem was not Sophiatown. It didn't exist on the cusp of destruction, hungry and frenetic in its struggle to outrun an entire government bearing down upon it. And maybe most strangely of all for a South African, the famous black neighbourhood had no clearly delineated boundaries. Unlike the carefully marked borders that divided blacks from whites in Johannesburg, Harlem's edges were amorphous, swallowed into the wider expanses of the city. What was more, the African Americans he met in Harlem were no *Drum* crowd. In a bookstore one afternoon, a clerk showed him a photograph of a lynching. From a description later given by Harold, the image was almost certainly of the well-known Omaha lynching of 1919. In the famous photograph of that murder, Nat saw a black man's corpse engulfed in flames, his body laid over a pile of twigs like kindling, the skin mottled and crisped nearly beyond recognition. Behind him, the crowd was captured in a moment of chilling mirth, posing behind the victim in open-mouthed delight. For days after he saw the photograph, Nat later told friends, he couldn't dislodge the image from his memory. South Africa, for all its history of oppression and racial violence, did not have a tradition of lynching, and that peculiar American institution was entirely foreign to him.[31]

Seeing the photograph of the lynching, however, was only one of the ways in which Harlem forced Nat to grapple with the same challenging fact that he and Harold had discussed earlier in the year – that black Americans lived lives completely different from his own. In Harlem, above all, he seems to have been struck again and again by the ways in which black Americans felt the possibilities of rising through their society, in a way that black South Africans living under apartheid could not. Their protests, by and large, were aimed at incorporating themselves into the wider folds of American society – and all that it promised – instead of claiming that society as their own.

However, if black America was not black South Africa, and Harlem was not Soweto, the neighbourhood still had peculiar charms that made it feel a bit like the places in which he had grown up. In Harlem he witnessed the 'filth and squalor' of a township, the same 'dirty hovels' passing for houses. 'I feel more at home in Harlem than I could ever be in the plush hotels downtown,' he wrote. 'A lot of Harlem's battles and preoccupations are no different from mine.' In an arresting image featured in the *New York Times* piece, he posed next to a large sign hanging from the bookstore window: 'THE

143

GOD DAM WHITE MAN' (*sic*). One day he waited for half an hour in the rain to find a taxi driver willing to take him into the neighbourhood. Whites, he noted almost proudly, were as afraid to go into Harlem as they were to go into Johannesburg's townships. Speaking opaquely of his own experience, he wrote in the *Times* that the people he met in the neighbourhood were 'like South African refugees who are desperate for a change back home but remain irrevocably in love with the country'.[32] For Nat it seemed the idea of home ran deeper than persecution.[33]

But when he returned to Cambridge, he found himself continually reminded of just how far he was from his own home. Beginning at the end of 1964 and continuing throughout the rest of Nat's time in the United States, student and community groups around Cambridge inundated him with requests to speak on the subject of the 'South African situation'.[34] These gatherings demoralised him, he confessed to his friend Kathleen Conwell, a young civil rights activist he met at Harvard, because they made him feel like a 'puppet dangling from a string', an act on display for the benefit of white liberals looking to assuage their own guilt.[35] He griped that it was easier to bring in a black South African to discuss the 'ferment in Southern Africa', as the Massachusetts League of Women Voters did at MIT in January 1965, than confront the racial upheaval sweeping through one's own country.[36]

That spring, Nat appeared on a made-for-TV documentary on the National Educational Television Network. 'South Africa: One Nation, Two Nationalisms' was a public television primer on the political crisis gripping South Africa. A booming

A Native of Nowhere

narrative voice guided viewers across the racialised landscape of National Party politics, coming to rest on the contentious issue of the first independent homeland, the Transkei. It introduced Nat as a 'young South African journalist who has visited the Transkei frequently and studied its problems'. As with his other public speaking engagements, Nat could not avoid being labelled as not simply a single voice in the debate, but the embodiment of an entire population. 'Nat Nakasa', the narrator explained, 'epitomizes the bitterness of the majority of Africans.'[37] As with his other stabs at public intellectualism, Nat's irritation at being made the mascot of a nation did not stop him from using the forums he was given to issue pointed critiques at his country. 'The Transkei is intended to serve as an excuse for the government to do what it pleases with Africans,' he explained coolly. Eight thousand miles from Johannesburg, he could finally make that relatively benign statement without fear that it would land him in jail or worse.

That didn't mean, however, that Nat had nothing to worry about when it came to his legal status in his new home. Although the INS had granted him an extension of his initial visa that still left him little time to manoeuvre himself into a more stable immigration situation. On 22 January 1965, he visited the INS office in Boston to ask if he might be able to travel to and from England, where a large community of South African exiles, including several *Drum* writers, resided. He also pushed to know what would happen when August came around. Would his visa be renewed again? But the answer from the INS was decisive and simple: he could not stay in the United States.[38]

The visit to the INS reinforced Nat's status as a kind of international refugee, stateless and forced to plead for the right to remain in any country. But his detailed questions about the length and flexibility of his visa also threw up a red flag for the INS official he spoke to that day. Two weeks later, she contacted the FBI in Boston to recommend they open a file on the South African writer. Her interview with Nat, she advised, would be 'of interest' to the local FBI branch.[39] In an era when the Bureau ran an extensive domestic surveillance campaign to watch and disrupt hundreds of activists and groups on the American left, including civil rights, feminist, anti-war, American Indian and student movement organisers, keeping tabs on Nat was most likely an obvious choice. The Boston FBI immediately enlisted sources at Harvard to dig deeper into Nat's past and life.

But the same week as the FBI opened their file on Nat, their longstanding surveillance of another controversial black figure came to a sudden end. On 21 February 1965, three members of the Nation of Islam stormed a stage in upper Manhattan where Malcolm X was delivering a speech and shot him sixteen times. Supporters rushed him to a nearby hospital, where doctors pronounced him dead on the scene.[40] Four months after Nat and the black nationalist leader talked pan-Africanism in Dar es Salaam, Malcolm X had been felled by his own disgruntled former supporters. For those following the trajectory of black activism in the United States, there was perhaps no more poignant indicator of how complicated and splintered it had become. 'The fact that Malcolm was what he was, and that he was allowed to be [that man] spoke well ... for the United States,' Nat told the *Harvard Crimson* three days later. 'But the fact that he was killed in this way will detract from that credit.'[41] For Nat, the assassination seemed to be yet another painful reminder that race relations in the United States could be just as bruising and deadly as they were in South Africa.

At the same time, Nat had once again turned a critical eye on his home country. Just after the winter break, in early 1965, a black student organisation at Princeton invited him to campus to give a talk about South Africa. Sitting in the front row that day was Harry Mashabela, a friend of Nat's from Johannesburg, who was at Princeton on another fellowship. Harry hadn't seen Nat since they'd left South Africa, and he was floored by his friend's changed demeanour. From his pulpit Nat delivered an angry screed about the liberation movement in South Africa. Too many blacks, he said, had been complacent in the apartheid system, lulled into submission by their own desire to just get on with their lives. He should know, he told the students, because he was among them. But he'd come to see he had been living a whitewashed existence. 'At home, when black people eat their meat without fully cooking it, it's called barbarous,' he said. 'Here in America, a white person can take their meat red, almost bleeding, and they call that a delicacy.' Harry sat back stunned. Nat 'was very bitter and very radical', he said. 'This was not the Nat I knew.'[42]

But this was not an anomaly, it seemed. Early in 1965, Nat

Stillman, an energetic freshman active in the school's SDS chapter, approached Nat about getting involved with an anti-apartheid campaign he was organising on campus. Part of a national SDS programme of anti-war and pro-working class actions, Stillman and students from SDS chapters in a few other cities had planned a series of speeches and protests to compel US companies to sever their financial ties with South African firms. Perhaps relieved to use his token status finally in the service of a political purpose, Nat agreed to act as a speaker for the campaign.

Although timed to mark the fifth anniversary of the Sharpeville Massacre, the SDS anti-apartheid protests grew out of nearly two decades of American activism – primarily propelled by African American political leaders – around the issue of divestment from the apartheid regime. Almost since the inception of National Party rule, activists within the American left had rallied around the idea that the United States should break political and financial ties with the repressive state.[43] But for the White House, the National Party government remained an important ally in southern Africa, a bulwark against the supposedly growing menace of communism in Africa. Despite a UN resolution calling for global sanctions in 1962, the Americans remained unmoved. By the time Nat Stillman began to plan his protests in the spring of 1965, frustrated activists had decided that if their government wouldn't enforce sanctions against the apartheid state, at the very least the American people could fight the National Party with their own chequebooks.

Early in March, mimeographed copies of a handwritten

SDS leaflet began circulating on Harvard Yard, announcing a demonstration against 'U.S. partnership in apartheid' on 19 March. A three-page memo written by Stillman accompanied the flyer, detailing how in the wake of brutal massacres and mass politically oriented arrests in South Africa, the United States unflaggingly maintained its support for the regime. But SDS, along with the Congress for Racial Equality and the Student Nonviolent Coordinating Committee, he wrote, would not be party to the suffering of millions of black South Africans. Their numbers were small, Stillman admitted, and the immorality of American investment would likely continue beyond their protests, but 'it is time that its practitioners know that *we* notice *them*; that the *we* is expanded and the *them* increasingly isolated' (emphasis in original).[44]

As the demonstration approached, SDS called on Nat to drum up support for their cause around Boston. On 16 March, the writer led a discussion and film screening on campus concerning apartheid and American financial interests in South Africa.[45] Three days later, at Boston's historic Faneuil Hall, he joined the Harvard senior Aggrey Awori, a Ugandan and president of the East African Students' Organization, to decry Harvard's own indirect investments in South Africa. Their talks were followed by a presentation from the community organiser Noel Day, who ended his speech with a provocation for the audience. Every freedom movement, he told them, must begin in the streets.[46]

The following day, 19 March, in coordination with protests across the country, a hundred demonstrators marched on the First National Bank of Boston, the United Shoe Machinery

Company and the Kendall Company – three powerful local businesses with known financial ties to the apartheid regime. For five hours, the SDS contingent and their supporters peacefully picketed the companies.[47] Meanwhile, in New York City, five hundred more demonstrators, most of them also white students, filled the steps outside Chase Manhattan Bank. As they marched, chanting 'Racist policies must go', a contingent of the SDS students leading the picket met with Lawrence Marshall, the bank's vice-chairman. 'The bank does not take sides,' he told them curtly. But the message was clear – Chase Manhattan, much like the US government, had no interest in severing its profitable ties with South Africa.

Building on the momentum of the Boston protests, Nat left Boston the following day to speak at a conference in Washington DC on the 'South African crisis and American action'. Headlined by keynote addresses from Oliver Tambo, the ANC's deputy president in exile, the American labour leader Victor Reuther and the civil rights leader James Farmer, the conference brought together delegates from a wide swathe of academia, government and the civil rights movement for three days of strategising on anti-apartheid activism. Nat, most likely accompanied by students from SDS – which helped organise the conference – had been invited to present on the subject of 'policies and activities of groups within South Africa'.[48]

That rather bland headline belied an apparently incendiary talk, at least in the eyes of the South African authorities.[49] The following week, the South African ambassador in Washington cabled his country's police commissioner to report that

'Nathaniel Nakasa, a bantu from South Africa ... spoke in an exaggerated and emotional fashion' at the conference. 'His main objective', the ambassador continued, 'was to lampoon certain situations in South Africa.'[50] The same week, the FBI special agent surveying Nat from the American end, also noted that the writer had recently participated in demonstrations against the apartheid state.[51] In a single three-day span, he had managed to pose a challenge to the authorities of both the country that had pushed him out and the one that had taken him in.

But whereas the idea of his rhetoric inflaming two governments might once have delighted Nat, the speeches in Cambridge and Washington only left him deeply embittered. The following week he brusquely explained in the *Harvard Crimson* that appealing to the immorality of apartheid could not destroy it. 'What happens in South Africa will be determined by power, not by who's right or wrong,' he told the reporter. And the problem lay not only with policies of white supremacy, he continued. South Africans themselves were 'too concerned about having a good time and getting along' to effectively challenge the state. Far from home, he seemed to be taking an indirect swipe at his own life in Johannesburg, which he was coming to see as weak-kneed and ineffectual. But he could do little more in the United States. Majority rule, he admitted glumly, would 'come all right – someday. But not for a long, long time.'[52]

Shortly after the Washington conference, Nat left Cambridge once again on a reporting trip for the *New York Times* magazine, this time to Alabama. The goal of the piece, like the Harlem essay, was to record his impressions of an unfamiliar place. As an outsider and a black South African, how did he see a southern state in the aftermath of massive civil rights protests? As so often before in both South Africa and the United States, Nat was meant to serve as a roving eye, an astute observer who could make his readers see something new in a well-worn subject matter.

This time, however, the project did not go as planned. Between 4 and 10 April 1965, Nat travelled to Alabama with the photographer Peter Magubane, presumably conducting interviews and taking down notes of what he saw.[53] But as the trip ended, he initially found himself too shaken to write about it. When he returned to Cambridge, he wrote a long letter to Allister Sparks, his former editor at the *Rand Daily Mail*, which gave Allister the impression that he was 'very troubled'.[54] Kathleen Conwell recalled that it was as though 'something had broken inside him'. For the first few days he was back in Cambridge, the two of them talked constantly about the trip. It had been heart-wrenching, Nat confessed, to see a place where black people had been so effectively stripped of their identity. 'In South Africa we have a culture that has lasted for generations; we have a language; we are a people,' he told her. 'But they took everything from you.'[55] Raw in his anger at this stifling of black America, he at last sat down to write the piece.

But the story continued to prove exceedingly difficult.

Weeks later, his editors returned his first draft with a request for a rewrite. He confessed to Ray that he couldn't decide if he should do it. What he had written was his honest account of the things he had seen, and a revision might blunt that. It seemed almost disingenuous to write anything else.[56]

On a journalistic level, however, Nat took the rejection of his writing hard. In the aftermath of Nat's editor's sharp words, Hugh Masekela watched him become even more dejected than he had already been in the United States, fearful that his days as a successful writer were coming to an end. 'He felt that he had lost it or just never had it,' Hugh remembered.[57] That spring, he also fumbled on an assignment for *Esquire*, a personal essay on his impressions of American women.[58] With his track record blemished, no new assignments were forthcoming.

Meanwhile, the Nieman fellowship raced toward its end. In the final weeks of the fellowship, Ray later remembered, Nat expressed increasing homesickness. He mused often about his 'raucous and carefree days' as a staff writer for *Drum* and appeared increasingly distraught about his prospects for the future. That May, the two men met one last time to say goodbye at a French coffee shop near Harvard Square. Ray was headed back to Alabama to continue reporting on civil rights, Nat to New York, where he knew several other South Africans in exile. But he wouldn't stay in the United States for long, he told his friend. He was considering heading north to Canada when his visa ran out in August, and he hoped to go back to Africa eventually, if not to South Africa then to Tanganyika. There perhaps he could start up another little magazine and smuggle it into the townships of Jo'burg.[59]

Nat's last goodbye at Harvard that spring went to the Nieman programme itself. In a final report penned for the foundation, he wrote that his time at the university had revealed its importance to him slowly, but by the time he left he knew both what he valued about academic life and what he could not stand. Studying race as an academic pursuit, he wrote, frustrated him immensely. 'I was apt to respond with a scream to disagreeable views, a disastrous tendency in any scholarly pursuit,' he told the programme. But his perspective on university life had not been entirely dark. What he had enjoyed most were 'those seminars in which human beings were discussed in a context of one human family'.[60]

With that final report complete, Nat left Cambridge and moved south to a place he had once characterised as 'the most indescribable place I have ever seen', Harlem.[61] There, he settled into an apartment at 151 Lenox Avenue, only three miles from the spot where Malcolm X had been assassinated less than four months before. But he couldn't settle into life in the city. For the first time since he had been in the United States, all around him swirled a small but close-knit community of South Africans he knew – Hugh Masekela and his sister Barbara, Miriam Makeba, Nimrod Mkele and the musician Caiphus Semenya, among others. Jack Thompson, his benefactor for *The Classic*, lived not far south of his neighbourhood, in a plush apartment overlooking Central Park. This collection of friends and acquaintances, however, all possessed jobs, steady projects and an assured immigration status. Twenty-eight years old, with a visa set to expire in less than three months and no offers of new writing projects, Nat had none of that, and little to anchor him in the foreign city.

That summer in Harlem, Nat became increasingly reclusive, prone to solitary drinking. In the city he had once called 'a great, modern slum', his friends watched helplessly as he slid back into a shadowy depression. 'He told all of us how unhappy he was,' Hugh said, 'but we couldn't hold him.'[62] At one point, Nadine Gordimer came through New York to meet with her publisher, and remembered the shock of seeing her old friend so levelled by his sadness. He seemed mentally hobbled, desperate to commit to a more radical politics but unwilling to renounce entirely the fringe country he'd left behind. He said he was frustrated that his friends in America couldn't understand why he'd associate with a white South African writer, whoever she was. And what was more, Nat confessed, the spectre of his mother's mental illness lurked around him constantly, and he feared he was going the same way.[63]

One day in July, Allister Sparks received two telegrams from Nat in rapid succession, one-liners that said simply, 'I need to speak with you.' But there was no phone number, no return address. 'I didn't even know where to start [to find him],' Allister remembered.[64] That same week, Hugh and Miriam invited Nat to go with them to see a play starring Diana Sands, a popular African American actress who was a close friend of Miriam's. On the evening of the performance, 13 July, the couple agreed to meet Nat in front of the theatre. But as the hour of the show approached, he still hadn't shown up, and they reluctantly went inside without him.[65]

Later that night, Jack Thompson was home in his Central Park West apartment when he received a call from a mutual friend of his and Nat's. The South African writer was in Harlem, 'very disturbed and talking about suicide'. Could Thompson come and calm him down? He immediately drove to Harlem and collected his young friend. When they got back to Jack's apartment, he poured them each a drink and the two men began to talk. Nat told him he was terrified that he was 'doomed to be mentally ill' like his mother, and didn't know if he could fight it. And more practically, he confessed he was in dire financial straits, jobless and nearly completely out of money. But after an hour or two of conversation, Jack remembered that Nat seemed calmer, more relaxed, and he offered to let him stay the night in his guest bedroom. Then, exhausted by the evening's ordeal, Jack went off to bed himself.[66]

Suddenly a persistent pounding on his front door jarred him awake. When he opened it, a police officer was standing in the entrance. Nat's body was lying on the sidewalk, seven storeys down. He had been in the United States for less than ten months. He was not yet 30 years old.

Two days later, a stunned group of Nat's friends and acquaintances gathered at the Frank Campbell Funeral Home on 81st Street for a quiet service. Nat's youngest brother, Moses, then a student in England, was the only member of his family in attendance. The sudden death had sent ripples of

A Native of Nowhere

grief through every community that had known him, from the Niemans to the *Drum* writers, but perhaps no one was harder hit than his fellow South African exiles in the United States, who knew too well the experience of being pushed out of their home country by circumstances far beyond their control.

At Nat's memorial service, one of these exiles, Miriam Makeba, sang a Zulu song whose title reporters translated as 'The Faults of These Noble Men'.[67] But indeed, what she and the others in attendance that day mourned was not the death of a noble man, but of one who had been, in many ways, quite ordinary. Like them, he had swept through apartheid South Africa as a young man, taking as much as he could from a state that gave little, conquering reporting assignments, women and the literary scene because he was a smart, ambitious man who saw what he wanted, and no reason why he should not have it. And like them, he had left his country not so much to take a principled stand but because it was the best option for his life and career, or so it had once seemed. 'We all cried,' remembered Hugh Masekela. 'He was the first … in exile [with us] to die and … I think part of the crying was out of the realisation that we all might die overseas.'[68] That kind of death, Hugh realised, was not noble at all, but tragic and unseemly.

The day after his funeral, friends buried Nat in Ferncliff Cemetery outside New York City, just feet from the spot where Malcolm X had been interred five months earlier, and not far from the grave of the black American novelist James Baldwin. Back in Durban, Chamberlain Nakasa told a local newspaper, 'the book is closed about my son: he is buried in America.'[69] With Nat gone, questions swirled about what had

157

pushed him to it, and many moved quickly to blame apartheid for the loss. If not for exile, they reflected bitterly, if not for the racism and repression that had forced him out of South Africa to begin with, Nat Nakasa would still be alive. 'We have paid again,' raged the South African playwright Athol Fugard. 'Let us make no mistake; this was another instalment in the terrible price and South Africa – that profligate spender of human lives – paid it.'[70] Even Nat himself had joked that exile from the apartheid state would be the end of him. 'After a lifetime of illegal living ... the exiles are suddenly called upon to become respectable, law-abiding citizens,' he wrote shortly before leaving South Africa. 'For my part it would be an act of providence if I survived under such circumstances.'[71] Indeed, it seems the sobering reality of life without apartheid was that it did not undo Nat's feeling that the world was a tremendously unjust place, but it left him wholly without a way to make sense of that injustice, and without a party to pin the blame on.

In evaluating the reasons for Nat's death, much has also been made of Nat's mother Alvina, and her own depression. But there may also have been another, more immediate cause for Nat's panic. On 1 July, just two weeks before his death, the FBI noted that immigration services had plans to contact Nat in the 'near future' and ask him to 'advise [the] agency of his plans for the future'. No follow-up information on the visit remains, but if it happened, it would have been an extremely upsetting moment for the young writer, whose time legally left in the United States could by that point be measured in days. Two weeks later, the FBI updated his file with a brief notation that the subject had ended his life. 'On the basis of [this] information, Boston [branch of the FBI] has placed this case in a closed status.'[72] Tailed actively by one government or another since he was 21, in death Nat was finally done with being spied upon.

In the days after the funeral, Nat's brother Moses stayed with Miriam and Hugh in their apartment in New Jersey, under the close watch of his brother's friends. Those who saw him in those days said Moses was clearly grieving, but not destroyed. 'He didn't seem to me like this thing had devastated him,' said Willie Kgositsile. 'I mean, it was no cause for celebration but it seemed that he would recover.'[73] But then, just as quickly as he had arrived in the United States for the funeral, Moses was gone, and his family would never see him again.

If the last days of Nat's life are difficult to reconstruct, the same period of his brother's life is even more opaque. Just after Nat left for the US in late 1964, Moses had apparently set off for Oxford to study political science. There, his story begins to disintegrate. Francie Suzman recalled picking up her phone one day to hear a black South African accent on the other end. The voice on the line introduced himself as Moses, Nat's baby brother. He was newly arrived in London, he said. Could he come by for tea sometime? They met, she said, just once. She didn't speak to him again. Nadine Gordimer also remembered meeting Moses when she passed through the UK, and was impressed by his 'keen mind'.

But after Nat's funeral, Moses seems to have disappeared. He never again contacted his family, who told me that they thought he had gone to the Congo to be part of the political ferment in that newly independent country. Other rumours surfaced as well. Miriam later told Nat's nephew that she thought Moses had gone off to Liberia. Alf Kumalo insisted that he actually met Moses in France just after Nat's death.

'What was he doing in France?' I asked. Alf's eyes grew distant.

'I don't know,' he said, 'but I remember I took portraits of him.'

Even the South African security police had an opinion. Deep in Nat's file is a note stating that he had a younger brother working for the PAC in Dar es Salaam.

But while Nat trailed paper evidence of his movements wherever he went – a newspaper column here, a police surveillance file there – Moses left behind almost no written trace. The South African police had no security file on him. He never applied for a passport. Neither Oxford nor Cambridge, the two universities that surviving friends insist he was studying at, has any record of a student by his name. Like so many of apartheid's victims, the greatest indignity about his disappearance is how quickly it faded from view, and how difficult it is, all these years later, to reconstruct even the most basic of facts about him. 'That's one of the many tragedies of this country,' Francie told me. 'These people who went into exile and then just vanished. And they vanished from memory, so they have died in every way possible.'

Eight months after Nat's death, *The Classic* published a commemorative issue in honour of its founder, titled simply 'The World of Nat Nakasa'. The magazine's pages were filled with Nat's writing, revealing once more his observant voice, his keen eye for nuance and gradient, his deep attachment to the people and places he covered. The articles it contains also paint a man conflicted, at once fiercely proud of his identity as a black South African and pained by the problems it occasioned, simultaneously angry at the world apartheid created and darkly amused, both a patriot and a deserter. As Nadine Gordimer explained, Nat 'wrote only of what was real to him ... accepting without embarrassment all the apparent contradictions in the complexity of his reaction to his situation, and ours – black and white'.[74] His journalism and his life came together not in a linear narrative but as a thousand tangled threads, not all of them proud, not all of them easy to make sense of.

But that Nat, the one whose life always teetered precariously on the edge of legality and common sense, could find no place in the United States. At Harvard, there was no fringe country, no community of people he could tap into who were living out a struggle against injustice in every moment of their daily lives. Instead, in Cambridge he found that he was seen as South Africa itself, a walking incarnation of his country, a one-man reservoir for everything it contained – even as that country itself disowned him. In the ten months Nat spent in the United States, that responsibility, and that hypocrisy, slowly undid him.

That Nat's life ended so early was not inevitable, but it was wrapped up in many factors he could not control – the terms of his exile, the mental health of his mother and, perhaps most importantly, the loneliness of being thousands of miles from his home, without even his identity as a citizen of South Africa to fall back on. 'On my side of the colour line, the easiest thing to do is to sink into despair,' Nat once wrote.[75] Yet until the very end of his life he fought this fate intensely, not through the political channels that many South Africans chose, but simply by leading a life that refused to remain within the bounds of the categories he fell into – black, South African, journalist, Nieman fellow. But never fully belonging had not always been his choice, and it had made quite frequently for a difficult life.

Five days after Nat died in New York, Ingrid Jonker, a widely read liberal Afrikaans poet, walked into the ocean off a picturesque beach in Cape Town and drowned herself. Just two years older than Nat, Ingrid came from a world that overlapped significantly with his own, and the spectre of their twin suicides became a marker of the profound destruction apartheid had wrought on South Africa's artistic and intellectual community.

Indeed, the hope for a different South Africa that fringe country had built up in township bars and back-alley jazz joints had little place in the country Nat and Ingrid had left behind. And the culture of writing and intellectualism that they had helped to cultivate was slowly dying of the wounds inflicted upon it by the National Party. Shortly after the publication of 'The World of Nat Nakasa', the government banned a final wave of *Drum* writers, and the editors had to go through the magazine with a razor-blade and slice out a tribute to Nat by his friend Can Themba, who had been silenced as a 'statutory communist'.[76] Can himself would die only two years later in 1968 from the effects of his alcoholism, in exile in Swaziland, and the renowned composer and *Drum* writer Todd Matshikiza passed away under similar circumstances the same year in Zambia. All four writers, Nat, Ingrid, Can and Todd – along with the countless others forced into exile or silence by National Party rule – had tried to speak around and through apartheid. But brilliant and fast-talking as they were, they all eventually found that their words could not outpace a government on a warpath, or the destruction it wrought. For Nat in particular, the undoing of that multiracial underground artistic culture that he had so loved left him on uncertain footing. But for those who knew him, his writing and his life also left glimmers of possibility for a new South Africa to come. As Nadine wrote, 'he belonged not between two worlds, but to both. And in him, one could see the hope of one world. He has left that hope behind; there will be others to take it up.'[77]

Conclusion

SO WHAT REALLY HAPPENED TO Nat Nakasa?

Here is what we know: On a warm July morning, he plunged to his death from a seventh-storey window of Jack Thompson's apartment near Central Park. He was taken to nearby Knickerbocker Hospital in West Harlem, where he was pronounced dead on arrival. In terse and clinical terms, his death certificate describes his condition: Multiple fractures and internal injuries. Fall from height. Undetermined circumstances. Pending police investigation.

That investigation, however, did not last long. Four days later, a detective submitted a short report on the death. Describing him as a 'male, Negro, age 28 years', the investigator wrote that Nat 'jumped or fell' from the open window at 9.10 a.m. on 14 July. When asked by the police, Jack Thompson repeated his story: he'd invited 'the deceased' to stay overnight at his house because 'he had been despondent' and Jack wanted to talk to him. The two spoke at length, before Jack headed off to bed for the night. The next thing he knew, he told the police, he was being awoken by a commotion – Nat's body was lying in the street.

The detective also spoke to Hugh Masekela, who said that Nat had confessed thoughts of suicide to him two weeks before, 'because he was finished'. That, apparently, was enough information for the investigator. 'The assigned found no evidence of foul play and that the subject apparently jumped,' he wrote. 'In view of the above, request that this case be marked closed.'[1] Notice of the death was sent to Nat's brother Moses in London and the investigation was officially marked complete.

But for many who knew Nat, that was hardly the end of the story. In the aftermath of his death, strange stories began to circulate. Shortly before he died, several people heard, he'd slaughtered a sheep near Harvard to exorcise the demons he believed had stalked him to the United States. In another often-retold rumour, he stumbled zombie-like up the down escalator of a New York subway station, unable to figure out where he was going. People spoke of depressed, drunken late-night phone calls from him, of strange rants he delivered about black power and the revolution in South Africa in a voice that seemed eerily unfamiliar and unlike the Nat they had once known.[2]

For many who knew Nat, his brisk decline and sudden death also became a kind of metaphor for the larger experience of exile. Willie Kgositsile, a young South African poet living in exile in the United States, remembered suddenly falling over as he approached the church where Nat's funeral was being held. He stood up, walked a few steps further on, and fell again. 'I tried it three or four times, then I gave up and left,' he told me. 'It was just that, I think, psychologically, there was such a resistance to going to a funeral service of anyone from home.'[3]

Back in Johannesburg, Juby Mayet remembered her own strange experience the day Nat died. The previous night, she said, she had a vivid dream in which she walked into the *Drum* office for work and there, at his desk as in the old days and grinning, was Nat Nakasa.

'What are you doing here?' she asked him.

'Juby,' he said, 'I'm home.'

The next morning when she awoke and went to work, she heard the news. 'I got shivers, goosebumps,' she told me. 'It's like Nat was saying to me [in my dream], I'm on my way home now.'[4]

The stories told about Nat's death speak not just to his final days, but to the physical and mental terrain that those who loved him have crossed in the years since. During the darkest decades of apartheid, as the system sprawled through the long years of the 1970s and 1980s, South African artists and writers would become wearily familiar with the experience of hearing that one of their own had died in exile, a victim of depression or drink or simply the startling darkness of never being able to go home. But in 1965, this was not yet the case. Nat was perhaps the first of this community to die abroad, causing many to remember his death with a vividness and sharp anger that have barely faded in the intervening decades.

What's more, because Nat's depression was so foreign to the experience most people had of him during his life, his death was suspicious from the start. 'Nat wasn't down and out,' his friend Alf Kumalo told me. To be sure, exile had stripped him of a great deal, but it was also a tremendous opportunity. 'I hung out with a hell of a lot of exiles. They could take it … They were free to do whatever they liked abroad, to live out their ambitions. So this life was quite okay.'[5] Many who knew Nat can rattle off a list of explanations for why he too should have been fine: he had contacts with American writers, he had friends around him, he could have gone to England or Botswana or Zambia, as many other South African exiles did. There were options for him, there was no reason to believe death was his only option.

On a warm October day in 2011, sitting in a strip mall in Durban, his sister told me her own view in no uncertain terms. 'Nat didn't jump,' she said. 'He was pushed.' When I asked how she knew, anger flashed in her eyes. 'I know he wouldn't have done that,' she said tersely. After all, here was the brother who for years had been the family's rising star, a journalist of growing fame who sent home a sum of money to the family each month and kept a watchful eye on his baby brother, Moses, as he went off to study in England. The year Nat died, he'd been at the apex of his career, and he knew he had a family back home nervously awaiting his return. Given all that, Gladys said, there was no way that he would have considered taking his own life.

Then what happened to him? Over the years, several theories about Nat's death have calcified into rumours, becoming well known among those who moved in his social circles. Some claim, for instance, that Nat discovered that

Jack Thompson's Farfield Foundation was CIA-funded and confronted him about it on that July night. The two fought, the story goes, and then Jack pushed him. (Both Jack and his wife, who was also in the apartment the night Nat died, have since passed away.) Others say an agent of the South African or American government had been sent to finish him off because his writing and speaking had ultimately proved too dangerous for their liking. Several have even suggested that a prickly and competitive colleague of Nat's at *Drum* was behind the death – that he'd been employed by the South African government to work as a kind of double-agent spying on his dissident friends. But in all of these explanations, it is hard to separate the historical reality from our contemporary understanding of it, to reach across the intervening decades without grazing the scars they have left behind. In Nat's legacy, as in anyone's, the past and present slump against each other, and it is hard to make out the space between them.

Over the years, these rumours have all acquired a strange velocity, and there has been little to stop them from careering in a score of different directions, each more tenuous than the last. Ultimately, however, this is a story told largely in its silences.[6] Forty-eight years after Nat's death, much about it is simply unknowable. Indeed, even after studying Nat's life for two years, I still think that as much as anyone can say about Nat's death is succinctly summed up in a letter to the editor of *Ilanga lase Natal* from July 1965. 'I am angry with Nat,' the letter writer opined. 'I want to say, "Nat, you damn fool. Why did you do it?" ... But ... it is our Government who made Nat homeless ... and whatever other reasons there may have been for his death, the fact that he could no longer return to his own country was, I am certain, a contributory factor. As far as I am concerned, Nat's death – at the age of 28 – will always be a stain, a blood stain, on the hands of White South Africa.'[7]

On 30 June 2009, South African President Jacob Zuma stood before a room of dignitaries at Durban's beachfront Elangeni Hotel to deliver the keynote address for the annual Nat Nakasa Award for Media Integrity. Given by the South African National Editors' Forum (SANEF) each year since 1998, the prize honours a journalist whose work shows a commitment to telling important and dangerous stories, regardless of the political trends of the day.[8] Facing the crowd of writers, editors and political dignitaries in the audience that night, Zuma lauded the country's journalists. They were, he asserted, a 'vital partner' in protecting and strengthening South Africa's young democracy. And staring into the past, he conjured up the name of the man who had inspired the award he was presenting. 'This evening,' he told the audience, 'you are celebrating the struggle of Nat Nakasa, and many other courageous journalists like him, against a political system that sought to silence them.'[9]

But only a year later, the president found himself squaring off against the very journalists he had praised that evening in Durban. In July 2010, following a series of embarrassing press revelations about corrupt deals orchestrated by Zuma's party, the African National Congress, the president announced plans to create a government-run media tribunal to punish journalists who published material considered to be slander or libel. That same winter, the party began aggressively pushing a new law that 'in the national interest' would classify broad swathes of governmental information as 'out of reach' of the press. The South African people, the ANC wrote in a policy memo, 'need recourse when media freedom trample[s] their rights to dignity and privacy'.[10] For the country's writers, however, these decisions signalled not so much a protection of South Africa's interests as an unabashed and eerily familiar attack on press freedom.

As the press and the government locked horns over freedom of speech and expression, both sides called upon the legacy of Nat Nakasa to support their cause. Although the writer had never been a major figure in South African history, his association with the SANEF award lent him significant currency in the debate. Minister of Justice Jeff Radebe told the members of SANEF that the new press regulations would protect the country's citizens – journalists included – from the dangers of misinformation, helping to create a media landscape that was a 'fitting tribute to departed gallant fighters such as Nat Nakasa'.[11] But Radebe's Nat Nakasa also had to contend with the Nat Nakasa conjured up by critics of the government's policy. As the Oxford professor Peter McDonald, a scholar of South African censorship, saw it, 'the ghost of Nat Nakasa' would haunt Parliament as it debated the new laws, 'because, as [he] insisted, the freedom of expression ... is an inalienable part of human dignity and a cornerstone of democracy'.[12] It seemed that wherever you stood in the debate,

A Native of Nowhere

Nat Nakasa could be used as a symbol, a lingering reminder of the scars apartheid had left on South African journalism, and a pervasive challenge to the country's contemporary society to avoid the mistakes of its past.

The fact that groups can use Nat's legacy today in such wildly divergent ways speaks, however, to a deeply troubling fact. Over the last four decades, popular memory has sapped his life story of nearly any substantive content, distilling it into little more than the fable of a man destroyed by the crushing weight of his country's injustice. As Pippa Green, a 1999 Nieman fellow from South Africa, noted, by dying so young and so far from home, 'Nat Nakasa has become the symbol of the loneliness of exile and of the struggle for dignity in racially oppressive societies'.[13] And it is not hard to see why. His biting anti-apartheid journalism, his meteoric rise to prominence and, most of all, his brisk and tragic end are the very stuff of which martyrdom is made.

But to think of Nat in this way misses an important truth: resistance to apartheid was acted out not by symbols but by people, zig-zagging through their lives without the moral clarity that historical hindsight affords. Such individuals are not simply shorthand for the injustices of apartheid – they are humans with sprawled and intricate lives that resist easy categorisation. The content of their experience must be filled in if we are ever to see apartheid in terms that extend beyond the tempting binaries so often applied to this period of South Africa's history: good and evil, black and white, oppressed and oppressor. And unfortunately for those who would make an idol of Nat Nakasa – or, indeed, Nelson Mandela, Desmond

Tutu, Steve Biko or any other prominent figure in the anti-apartheid movement – deification does not hold up well to the scrutiny of detail.

Instead, what emerges from studying Nat's life at close range is a far more complex narrative. Most basically, one witnesses the rise and fall of a talented and ambitious man whose life developed alongside a cruel system of racial hierarchy. But the link between his life and apartheid was not simple, nor was it static. Born before the National Party took power, he knew in his earliest years a South Africa where its rule was only one possibility among many. As for so many of his generation, his reaction to the National Party's ascendancy was coloured by the fact that he could easily envision a world without apartheid, since for eleven years he had actually lived in one.

Indeed, the 1948 election of the National Party marked a turning point – for his life and for his country – only in retrospect. For several years afterward, apartheid remained a developing vision, lacking both the rigidity and sense of permanence that would later come to define it. In many ways, it cohered only as people resisted it, not just through large-scale protests and strikes, but also through insidious, everyday challenges of the kind Nat so loved – going into a city without a pass, sleeping with white women, writing magazine articles about a multiracial fringe country. These small acts grated against the National Party's vision of a divided South Africa, forcing it to develop increasingly methodical means for snuffing out resistance over the course of the 1950s and 1960s.

But while apartheid drew the boundaries tighter and

tighter around Nat's personal and professional world, it also lent his life a powerful sense of purpose. Nat and other writers, intellectuals and activists of his generation defined themselves in large part by the fact that they moved outside the prescribed bounds of the apartheid state. Life on the fringe gave them their voice, lending a persistent feeling of urgency to both their careers and their personal lives. In a country where any day could be the one on which you were arrested, relocated, fired or censored, there was little point in living patiently. By the time Nat died at the age of 28, he had already worked for nine years as a journalist for several of South Africa's most prominent publications, founded a literary magazine and completed an internationally renowned fellowship at Harvard. Apartheid had forced him to move fast, blazing over hurdles that in another society would have taken decades to clear.

The narrative of Nat's dazzling rise to prominence in the midst of daunting obstacles is, however, incomplete if we do not also recognise that in many ways he was not particularly remarkable at all. He did not possess some innate level of bravery that pushed him to take on apartheid in the ways that he did – or, at the very least, there was something more to it than that. Above all, he lived as he did because circumstances necessitated it. His life was breathless, dangerous and courageous, because to be a writer in 1960s South Africa, one had no other choice. 'The writer can take his choice,' he once wrote, 'bow to social conventions ... and keep within the confines of the white world, or refuse to let officialdom regulate his personal life, face the consequences, and be damned.'[14]

Notes

Introduction

1 Nat Nakasa, 'Native of Nowhere', *The Classic* 1:1 (1963), 73.
2 Hugh Masekela, interview with the author, Chapel Hill, NC, 12 October 2010.
3 Jacob Dlamini, *Native Nostalgia* (Johannesburg: Jacana, 2009), 21.
4 Juby Mayet, interview with the author, Lenasia, May 2012.
5 Thabo Mbeki, Speech at the Launch of the African Renaissance Institute, Pretoria, 11 October 1999, accessed 29 March 2011, http://www.dfa.gov.za/docs/speeches/1999/mbek1011.htm.
6 Lelyveld, who went on to become the executive editor of the *Times*, won the Pulitzer Prize for his memoir of his work in South Africa. He was expelled by the apartheid government in the mid-1960s, allowed to return only two decades later. Joseph Lelyveld, *Move Your Shadow: South Africa, Black and White* (New York: Times Books, 1985), 25.
7 The exceptions to this trend are a small number of unpublished dissertations on Nat. They include Heather Acott, 'Tactics of the Habitat: The Elusive Identity of Nat Nakasa' (Unpublished Master's Thesis: University of South Africa, 2008); H.B. Singh, 'Nathaniel Nakasa, the Journalist as Autobiographer: A Crisis of Identity' (Unpublished Master's Thesis: University of Natal, 1990); Matthew

Keaney, "'I Can Feel My Grin Turn to a Grimace": From Sophiatown Shebeens to the Streets of Soweto on the Pages of *Drum, The Classic, New Classic,* and *Staffrider*' (Unpublished MA thesis, George Mason University, 2010); Margot Jacqueline Malebo Leger, 'Rediscovering *The Classic*: Voices of 1960s South Africa' (Unpublished Honours Thesis: Harvard University, 2013).

Chapter 1

1 Gladys Maphumulo, telephone interview with the author, 7 November 2010; Gladys Maphumulo, interview with the author, 5 October 2011.
2 'Cost of Coronation Heaviest in History', *New York Times*, 13 May 1937, 18.
3 Saul Dubow, 'Introduction: South Africa's 1940s', *South Africa's 1940s: Worlds of Possibilities*, ed. Saul Dubow and Alan Jeeves (Cape Town: Double Storey, 2005), 2.
4 Iain Edwards, 'Cato Manor: Cruel Past, Pivotal Future', *Review of African Political Economy* 21:61 (September 1994), 420.
5 Theo Zindela, *Ndazana: The Early Years of Nat Nakasa* (Braamfontein: Skotaville Publishers, 1990), 36.
6 Deborah Posel, *The Making of Apartheid* (Oxford: Clarendon Press, 1991), 34.
7 H.C. Brookfield and M.A. Tatham, 'The Distribution of Racial Groups in Durban: The Background of Apartheid in a South African City', *Geographical Review* 47:1 (1957), 49, 53.
8 Ibid., 53.
9 Walter Johnson, 'Education: Keystone of Apartheid', *Anthropology & Education Quarterly* 13:3 (Autumn 1982, 1982), 217; Stephen R. Lewis, *The Economics of Apartheid* (New York: Council on Foreign Relations Press, 1990), 23.
10 Sipho Nakasa, email message to the author, 3 September 2010.
11 Mark Gevisser, *A Legacy of Liberation: Thabo Mbeki and the Future of the South African Dream* (New York: Palgrave Macmillan, 2009), 27.

12 Ismail Meer, *A Fortunate Man* (Cape Town: Zebra Press, 2002), 27.
13 James T. Campbell, *Songs of Zion: The African Methodist Episcopal Church in the United States and South Africa* (New York: Oxford University Press, 1995), 305–10.
14 Chamberlain Nakasa, 'Gugu and Bajabulile Story and Their Design of the Pattern', *Ilanga lase Natal*, 16 February 1957.
15 Alan Paton, *Cry, the Beloved Country* (New York: Scribner, 2003), 7.
16 Chamberlain Nakasa, *The Gospel of Self Help* (Durban: Publisher unknown, 1941), 78.
17 Ibid., 76.
18 Ibid., 74.
19 Zindela, *Ndazana*, 1.
20 Gladys Maphumulo, telephone interview with the author, 7 November 2010.
21 Heather Acott, email message to the author, 15 July 2010; Nadine Gordimer, 'One Man Living Through It', *The Classic* 2:1 (1966), 14.
22 'Report of the Mental Hospitals Departmental Committee', as quoted in Robert R. Edgar and Hilary Sapire, *African Apocalypse: The Story of Nontetha Nkwenkwe, a Twentieth-Century South African Prophet* (Athens, OH: Ohio University, Center for International Studies, 2000), 55.
23 Zindela, *Ndazana*, 8; Sipho Nakasa, email message to the author, 3 September 2010; Edgar and Sapire, *African Apocalypse*, 33.
24 Gladys Maphumulo, telephone interview with the author, 7 November 2010.
25 'So, African Nationalists Seen Harder than Jan Smuts', *Atlanta Daily World*, 8 April 1948, 3.
26 'Racial Problem in South Africa: Signs of a More Liberal Native Policy', *The Scotsman*, 13 February 1948, 7.
27 A.J. Friedgut, 'South Africa: Election Year', *The Observer*, 9 May 1948, 4.
28 Ibid.
29 Robert Ross, *A Concise History of South Africa* (Cambridge: Cambridge

University Press), 123.
30 Quoted in Leonard Thompson, *A History of South Africa* (New Haven: Yale University Press, 2001), 186.
31 In the 2000s, Durban moved to change almost all of its street names – Warwick Avenue has since become Julius Nyerere Avenue, and Victoria Street is now Bertha Mkhize Street.
32 Still, the next morning, the local white newspaper led with a story about a storm in nearby Mossel Bay.
33 'Report of the Commission of Enquiry into Riots in Durban' (Union of South Africa, 1949), 4.
34 '53 Dead: 325 Hurt in Riots', *Natal Mercury*, 15 January 1949, 1.
35 'Stay at Home Appeal', *Natal Mercury*, 15 January 1949.
36 'Durban's Reign of Terror', *Cape Times*, 15 January 1949, 1; 'Zulu-Indian Casualties Rise as Rioting Spreads', *Los Angeles Times*, 17 January 1949, 1.
37 '53 Dead: 325 Hurt in Riots', *Natal Mercury*, 1.
38 'Commission of Enquiry into the Durban Riots'; Debates of the South African House of Assembly, Second Session – Tenth Parliament, 21 January to 30 June 1949, vol. 68, column 5840.
39 One 9-year-old white boy was also killed when a stray bullet struck him during a firefight. There were also a small number of victims whose race was not identified. 'Report of the Commission of Enquiry into Riots in Durban', 5.
40 'Zulu-Indian Riot Report Being Readied', *Atlanta Daily World*, 1 April 1949, 1.
41 'Durban a Sign for Malan: Smuts' Warning on Colour Policy', *Cape Times*, 17 January 1949, 2; 'Smuts Sounds Warning', *New York Times*, 16 January 1949, 26.
42 Meer, *A Fortunate Man*, 27.
43 Chamberlain Nakasa, *The Gospel of Self Help*, 88.
44 Hendrik Verwoerd, 'Bantu Education Act: Speech before Parliament, August 17, 1953', *Verwoerd Speaks: Speeches 1948–1966* (Johannesburg: APB Publishers, 1966), 83.

45 Obed Kunene, interview with A. Manson and D. Collins, 19 April 1979, KCAV 123, Killie Campbell Africana Library, Durban.
46 'Zulu Lutheran High School: Junior Certificate Result – 1954', *Ilanga lase Natal*, 5 February 1955, 15; South African Bureau of Statistics, *Population Census*, 6 September 1960 (Pretoria: Govt. Printer, 1963–70), 391–3.
47 It should be noted that these percentages are all based on official figures reported in the South African census. Brookfield and Tatham, 'The Distribution of Racial Groups in Durban', 46.
48 Ibid., 53.
49 Nat Nakasa, 'Oh, to Be an Anonymous Houseboy', *The Classic* 1:1 (1963), 60.
50 These laws included the 1950 Group Areas Act, the 1951 Native Laws Amendment Bill, the 1951 Prevention of Illegal Squatting Act, and the 1952 Abolition of Passes and Documents Act (which ironically required all Africans to carry a renamed pass called a 'reference book'). For a more detailed discussion of the individual pieces of legislation and their particular effects on apartheid urban population control policy, see Deborah Posel, 'Struggles over Influx Control Legislation', *The Making of Apartheid*, 90–115.
51 Ibid., 102.
52 Ibid., 120.
53 Zindela, *Nzadana*, 5.
54 Ibid., 17.
55 Ibid.
56 Enoch Duma, interview with the author, Roodepoort, 11 December 2011.
57 Zindela, *Nzadana*, 17.
58 'Cultural Club's Beginning', *Ilanga lase Natal*, 23 February 1957, 21; Nat Nakasa, 'Chesterville a Paradise for Vice Addicts', *Ilanga lase Natal*, 26 May 1956, 19.
59 Les Switzer, 'Bantu World and the Origins of a Captive African Commercial Press in South Africa', *Journal of African Studies* 14:3

(April 1988), 353.
60 Dube himself was a leading black reformer in early twentieth-century South Africa, and served as the first president of the South African Native National Congress, the forerunner of the country's current ruling party, the African National Congress. John Dube, 'Editor's Note', *Ilanga lase Natal*, 10 April 1903, quoted in R. Hunt Davis Jr., '"Qude Maniki!" John L. Dube, Pioneer Editor of Ilanga lase Natal', *South Africa's Alternative Press: Voices of Protest and Resistance, 1880–1960* (Cambridge: Cambridge University Press, 1997), 83.
61 Davis, 'Qude Maniki!', 357.
62 Zindela, *Nzandana*, 10–11.
63 Quoted in Switzer, 'Bantu World', 360.
64 'Ilanga Reporter is Arrested', *Ilanga lase Natal*, 9 February 1957, 1.
65 Sylvester Stein, *Who Killed Mr. Drum?* (Bellville: Mayibuye Books, 1999), 116.
66 Ibid., 115.
67 Ibid.
68 Joseph Nakasa, interview, *Nat Nakasa: A Native of Nowhere*, dir. Lauren Groenewald (Times Media South Africa, 1999), DVD.
69 Gordon H. Pirie, 'Rolling Segregation into Apartheid: South African Railways, 1948-53', *Journal of Contemporary History* 27:4 (October 1992), 681.

Chapter 2
1 Nat Nakasa, 'Johannesburg, Johannesburg', *The Classic* 2:1 (1966), 18.
2 Ibid.
3 Nat Nakasa, 'Fringe Country: Where There is No Colour Bar', *Drum*, March 1961, 23.
4 Nakasa, 'Johannesburg, Johannesburg', 19.
5 Lewis Nkosi, *Home and Exile* (London: Longmans, 1965), 4.
6 What had been Sophiatown was re-zoned as a white area and named 'Triomf', Afrikaans for 'triumph'. David Goodhew, *Respectability and*

Resistance: A History of Sophiatown (Westport: Praeger, 2004), xvi.

7 District Six remains perhaps the best-remembered emblem of the resistance to apartheid zoning policies. The interracial neighbourhood in the heart of Cape Town was subject to a massive forced removal between 1968 and 1982, which eventually expelled more than 60,000 residents from the area. But the long struggle over the area left the razed neighbourhood a contested ground, and aside from a technical college constructed on the land in the 1980s, it remains undeveloped even today. The empty fields of District Six cut a massive hole through the centre of the city, while the townships where its former residents were sent are scattered across the urban periphery, a lasting reminder of the power of apartheid housing policy.

8 Ulf Hannerz, 'Sophiatown: The View from Afar', *Journal of Southern African Studies* 20:2 (June 1994), 185.

9 Bloke Modisane, *Blame Me on History* (London: Thames and Hudson, 1963), 16.

10 Nkosi, *Home and Exile*, 40.

11 Mike Nicol, *A Good Looking Corpse* (London: Secker & Warburg, 1991), xii.

12 Ibid., 28.

13 Finding an African editorial staff, however, was no easy task in a country where the annual number of black university graduates could be counted in the hundreds, and in Sampson's view, white editors remained a necessity. They brought a level of journalistic expertise and experience that black South Africans simply could not gain within the confines of the country's racial hierarchy, at least not before *Drum* came around. Although the magazine's white ownership was not without controversy, and indeed frustrated many of its black writers, they also recognised that this management structure provided the magazine with the capital and social clout to launch their careers in a society intent on shutting such opportunities down.

14 'The Press: South African Drumbeats', *Time*, 15 December 1952, accessed 12 October 2010, http://www.time.com/time/magazine/

article/0,9171,820505,00.html.
15 Michael Chapman, 'More than Telling a Story: *Drum* and its Significance in Black South African Writing', *The Drum Decade: Stories from the 1950s* (Pietermaritzburg: University of Natal Press, 1989), 194–6.
16 Joe Thloloe, interview with the author, Johannesburg, November 2011.
17 'The Press: South African Drumbeats', *Time*.
18 Nicol, *A Good Looking Corpse*, 15.
19 Mari Snyman, 'Can Themba: The Life and Work of a Shebeen Intellectual' (Unpublished Master's Thesis: University of Johannesburg, 2007), 2.
20 Anthony Sampson, *Drum: An African Adventure – and Afterwards* (London: Hodder & Stoughton, 1956), 26.
21 Nat Nakasa, 'Writing in South Africa: A Speech at the University of the Witwatersrand', *The World of Nat Nakasa* (Johannesburg: Ravan Press, 1975), 80; R. Neville Choonoo, 'The Sophiatown Generation: Black Literary Journalism during the 1950s', *South Africa's Alternative Press*, 254; Nkosi, *Home and Exile*, 4–5; see also Tim Couzens, *The New African: A Study of the Life and Work of H.I.E. Dhlomo* (Johannesburg: Ravan Press, 1985).
22 All of the *Drum* writers were male, with a few prominent exceptions. Juby Mayet was a long-time female staff writer for the magazine. The internationally renowned Bessie Head was also an occasional *Drum* contributor. She left South Africa in 1964, and died in exile in Botswana in 1986. As will be discussed later in the chapter, the *Drum* culture was predicated in part on a certain, specific definition of masculinity, and generally made little space for female writers. In fact, at least in the early years of the magazine, even its advice column, 'Heartbreaks', published under the pseudonym 'Dolly Drum', was written by a man. See Sampson, *Drum: An African Adventure*, 97–101.
23 Suppression of Communism Act of 1950, reprinted in *Aluka*, accessed 16 September 2010, http://bit.ly/dzxcOG.
24 Daniel Kunene, 'Ideas under Arrest, Censorship in South Africa',

Research in African Literatures 12:4 (Winter 1981), 425
25 Mongane Serote, interview, *Nat Nakasa: A Native of Nowhere*.
26 Tom Hopkinson, *Under the Tropic* (London: Hutchinson Press, 1984), 31. Hopkinson was the editor of *Drum* between 1958 and 1961.
27 Can Themba, 'The Boy with the Tennis Racket', *The Classic* 2:1 (1966), 8.
28 Can Themba, *The Will to Die* (Cape Town: David Philip, 1972), 111; Peter Magubane, interview with the author, Johannesburg, 24 July 2012.
29 Joe Thloloe, interview with the author, Johannesburg, November 2011.
30 Leslie Sehume, interview with the author, Dube, Soweto, 8 February 2012.
31 Nkosi, *Home and Exile*, 20–1.
32 Leslie Sehume, interview with the author, Dube, Soweto, 8 February 2012.
33 Juby Mayet, interview with the author, Lenasia, 5 December 2011; Joe Thloloe, interview with the author, Johannesburg, November 2011.
34 Juby Mayet, interview with the author, Lenasia, 5 December 2011.
35 Ronald Suresh Roberts, *No Cold Kitchen: A Biography of Nadine Gordimer* (Johannesburg: Real African Publishers, 2005), 138.
36 Nat Nakasa, 'Snatching at the Good Life', *The World of Nat Nakasa*, 22.
37 Nakasa, 'Fringe Country', 23.
38 Nakasa, 'Johannesburg, Johannesburg', 5.
39 Ibid., 4.
40 Ibid., 5.
41 Ibid., 4.
42 Frances Jowell, interview with the author, Parktown, Johannesburg, 17 May 2012.
43 Ibid.; Leslie Sehume, interview with the author, Dube, Soweto, 8 February 2012; Nadine Gordimer, interview with the author, Parktown, Johannesburg, 19 April 2012.

44 Nakasa, 'Johannesburg, Johannesburg', 7.
45 Frances Jowell, interview with the author, Parktown, Johannesburg, 17 May 2012.
46 David Hazelhurst, interview with the author, Johannesburg, November 2011.
47 Nakasa, 'Johannesburg, Johannesburg', 5; Harry Mashabela, interview with the author, Pretoria, 10 February 2012.
48 Thabo Mbeki, interview with Mark Gevisser, 26 August 2000, South African History Archive, AL3284: Mark Gevisser's Research Papers for 'Thabo Mbeki: The Dream Deferred', X10–12.
49 Mark Gevisser, *Thabo Mbeki: The Dream Deferred* (Cape Town: Jonathan Ball, 2007), 138.
50 Nat Nakasa, 'Afrikaner Youth Get a Raw Deal', *The World of Nat Nakasa*, 61.
51 Enoch Duma, interview with the author, Roodepoort, 11 December 2011.
52 Lewis Nkosi, 'Review of *The World of Nat Nakasa*', *Research in African Literatures* 9:3 (1978), 478.
53 Ibid.
54 Advertisement, *The Star*, 18 April 1959, 10; Advertisement, *Rand Daily Mail*, 4 April 1959, 8; Advertisement, *The Star*, 16 January 1959, 17; Advertisement, *The Star*, 16 October 1959, 24.
55 Advertisement, *The Star*, 17 August 1959, 21; Advertisement, *The Star*, 2 December 1959, 33; Advertisement, *Rand Daily Mail*, 27 July 1959, 10.
56 Malcolm Purkey, Introduction, 'Sophiatown', *Drama for a New South Africa*, ed. David Graver (Bloomington: Indiana University Press, 2000), 25–6.
57 Enoch Duma, interview with the author, Roodepoort, 11 December 2011.
58 Purkey, 'Sophiatown', 65.

Chapter 3

1 Nat Nakasa, 'Do Blacks Hate Whites?' *Drum*, November 1958, 19.
2 David Hazelhurst, interview with the author, Johannesburg, November 2011; Allister Sparks, interview with the author, Rivonia, Johannesburg, 21 October 2011; Leslie Sehume, interview with the author, Dube, Soweto, 8 February 2012.
3 Joe Thloloe, interview with the author, Johannesburg, November 2011.
4 Nakasa, 'Afrikaner Youth Get a Raw Deal', 92.
5 Mongane Serote, 'The Nakasa World', *The World of Nat Nakasa*, xxxi.
6 Sampson, *Drum: An African Adventure*, 49.
7 Nakasa, 'Johannesburg, Johannesburg', 5.
8 South African Bureau of Statistics, *Population Census*, 391–3.
9 Nakasa, 'Johannesburg, Johannesburg', 5.
10 There were approximately 17,000 African men, out of a total population of approximately 2,860,000 adult males, with secondary school diplomas in 1960. Nat was not among them – he dropped out of school after Standard 8 (roughly the equivalent of 10th grade), placing him in the top 2 per cent of education levels among adult African men. South African Bureau of Statistics. *Population Census*, 391–3.
11 Modisane, *Blame Me on History*, 94.
12 Themba, 'Tennis Racket', 10.
13 The life of that boxer, Ezekiel Dlamini, later became the subject of the immensely popular South African jazz opera, *King Kong*, which was written, scored and acted by friends of Nat's and went on to international success. Nat Nakasa, 'Quite a Place, Fourteenth Street', *The World of Nat Nakasa*, 9; For articles mentioned in this paragraph, see Nat Nakasa, 'Why Taximen are Terrified', *Drum*, March 1958, 30–5; 'Look What We Drink', *Drum*, February 1958, 15–16; 'The Life and Death of King Kong', *Drum*, February 1959, 29–32.
14 Sampson, *Drum: An African Adventure*, 102.
15 Nat Nakasa, 'The Team That Came from Nowhere', *Drum*, September 1961, 40.

A Native of Nowhere

16 Nat Nakasa, 'The Fat Cigar: It's Their Badge of Success', *Drum*, November 1961, 54.
17 Nat Nakasa, 'Some Day We Will Be Back', *Drum*, February 1963, 21.
18 Ibid., 20.
19 Zindela, *Ndazana*, 18; Alf Kumalo, interview with the author, Diepkloof, Soweto, 28 November 2011.
20 Can Themba, 'Crepuscule', *The Will to Die*, 3.
21 1927 Immorality Act, reprinted in *Aluka*, accessed 20 October 2010, http://bit.ly/addpKO; 1950 Immorality Amendment Act, reprinted in *Aluka*, accessed 20 October 2010, http://bit.ly/dBZZFE.
22 Nkosi, *Home and Exile*, 12.
23 Peter Magubane, interview with the author, Johannesburg, 24 July 2012; Roseinnes Phahle, interview with the author, Killarney, Johannesburg, 1 August 2012.
24 Nadine Gordimer, interview with the author, Parktown, Johannesburg, 19 April 2012.
25 Barbara Bailey, interview with the author, Lanseria, Johannesburg, 21 December 2011.
26 Willie Kgositsile, interview with the author, Johannesburg, 21 May 2012; Juby Mayet, interview with the author, Lenasia, 5 December 2011.
27 Nat Nakasa, 'Must We Ride to Disaster?' *Drum*, October 1962.

Chapter 4

1 This account draws primarily on news coverage of the event published in the days following the massacre. However, some of the details of that day, including the size and composition of the crowd, and the number of people killed, are still under debate by historians. For further detail, see Philip Frankel, *An Ordinary Atrocity: Sharpeville and its Massacre* (New Haven: Yale UP, 2001); Ambrose Reeves, *Shooting at Sharpeville: Agony of South Africa* (New York: Houghton Mifflin, 1960); and Tom Lodge, *Sharpeville: An Apartheid Massacre and Its Consequences*

(Oxford: Oxford UP, 2011). 'South Africa Police Kill 62 Rioting Natives', *Chicago Daily Tribune*, 22 March 1960, 5; 'South Africa: The Sharpeville Massacre', *Time* , 4 April 1960, accessed 21 October 2010, http://www.time.com/time/magazine/article/0,9171,869441-1,00.html; 'They Must Learn the Hard Way', *The Guardian*, 22 March 1960, 1.
2 'The Tragedy at Sharpeville', *New York Times*, 22 March 1960, 36.
3 The exception to the trend of African independence movements was the southern end of the continent. Not only South Africa but also Mozambique, Angola and Southern Rhodesia (now Zimbabwe) remained under white rule through the 1970s. Mozambique and Angola became independent in 1975, and Zimbabwe in 1980. South West Africa (now Namibia) was administered by the Republic of South Africa until 1990 under a League of Nations mandate.
4 Nat Nakasa, 'The Human Meaning of Apartheid', *New York Times Magazine*, 24 September 1961, 46.
5 Ibid., 42.
6 The photographs themselves, however, were published in many international outlets, and helped drum up global outrage over the massacre.
7 Peter Magubane, 'Sharpeville Funeral', *Drum*, May 1960, 28–31.
8 Nat Nakasa, 'Over the Border', *Drum*, July 1960, 24–7.
9 Lewis Nkosi to Francie Suzman, 1 May 1960. In possession of author.
10 Nakasa, 'Apartheid', 44.
11 Lewis Nkosi to Francie Suzman, 1 May 1960.
12 Karin Shapiro, 'No Exit?: The Politics of Emigration Restrictions in Early Apartheid South Africa', *NEWSA Conference* (Unpublished article, April 2007), 16.
13 Nakasa, 'Apartheid', 47.
14 Tom Hopkinson, *In the Fiery Continent* (London: Victor Gollancz, 1962), 352, 293, 364.
15 'Priscilla Asks', *Drum*, July 1961, 73; 'Rhodesia: An Uneasy Time Ahead!', *Drum*, July 1961, 19; 'War or Peace?' *Drum*, October 1961,

82–3; 'Forward Tanganyika', *Drum*, December 1961, 33.
16 For examples of this, see Philip Kgosana, 'My Exciting Life', *Drum*, February 1961, 56–61; 'What the Leaders Say', *Drum*, June 1961, 21–3; Nat Nakasa, 'Where Do We Go from Here? Ask Treason Trialists', *Drum*, May 1961, 22–3, 79; 'Give Us a Say in S.A.', *Drum*, November 1961, 43; Albert Lutuli, 'If I Were Prime Minister', *Drum*, December 1961, 13–17.
17 Hopkinson, *In the Fiery Continent*, 346–9; Benson Dyantyi, 'The Earth Shakes in Pondoland', *Drum*, January 1961, 21–5; 'What the Leaders Say', *Drum*, June 1961, 21–3; Walter Ehmeir, 'Publishing South African Literature in English in the 1960s', *Research in African Literatures* 26:1 (Spring 1995), 123.
18 Prior to the end of World War I, South West Africa had been a German territory, and was the site of one of the first modern genocides, perpetrated by German troops against the Herero and Nama peoples between 1904 and 1907. See Sven Lindqvist, '*Exterminate All the Brutes': One Man's Odyssey into the Heart of Darkness and the Origins of European Genocide*, trans. Joan Tate (New York: The New Press, 1992).
19 National Archives, Pretoria, Department of Justice file for Nathaniel Nakasa, 1959–1965, 17. Translated by Kate Ryan.
20 Nat Nakasa and Dick Walker, 'Inside South West Africa', *Drum*, September 1961, 30–1.
21 Department of Justice file for Nathaniel Nakasa, 1959–1965, 17.
22 Nat Nakasa, 'Inside Mozambique Today: Freedom to Lose All', *Drum*, July 1962, 51.
23 Philip Kgosana (with Nat Nakasa), 'How I Got Out and Why', *Drum*, April 1962, 21.
24 Philip Kgosana, interview with the author, Pretoria, 9 January 2012.

Chapter 5
1 Themba, 'Tennis Racket', 9.
2 Ibid.

Ryan Brown

3 Nat Nakasa, 'Comment', *The Classic* 1:1 (1963), 4.
4 Suppression of Communism Act of 1950, reprinted in *Aluka*, accessed 16 September 2010, http://bit.ly/dzxcOG.
5 Department of Justice file for Nathaniel Nakasa, 1959–1965, 17.
6 Ehmeir, 'Publishing South African Literature', 113.
7 *Drum* had once published fiction as well, but stopped in 1958, when the editorship turned over from Sylvester Stein, a lover of short fiction, to the hardnosed Tom Hopkinson, who came from a news background and believed the magazine should focus strictly on journalistic forms of writing. Jim Bailey agreed, arguing that crime, sports and gossip sold the magazine, not literary copy. For further detail, see Ehmeir, 'Publishing South African Literature', 115; Chapman, 'More than Telling a Story', 216.
8 Nakasa, 'Comment', 4.
9 John Thompson to Nat Nakasa, 15 May 1962, Fol. B3, Nathaniel Nakasa Papers 1963–1984, University of the Witwatersrand, Historical Papers, Johannesburg.
10 From a Farfield Foundation informational brochure, quoted in Frances Saunders, *The Cultural Cold War: The CIA and the World of Arts and Letters* (New York: The New Press, 1999), 126.
11 Ibid., 2.
12 Ibid., 117; 'Arab Magazine Banned by Cairo', *New York Times*, 24 July 1966, 3.
13 For a more in-depth discussion of Cold War politics in Africa and the ideological motivations for involvement on the continent, see Odd Arne Westad, *The Global Cold War: Third World Interventions and the Making of Our Times* (Cambridge: Cambridge University Press, 2005).
14 Peter Benson. '"Border Operators": Black Orpheus and the Genesis of Modern African Art and Literature', *Research in African Literatures* 14:4 (1983), 442.
15 Ibid.
16 John Thompson to Nat Nakasa, 12 December 1962, Fol. B3, Nathaniel Nakasa Papers.

17 Lewis Nkosi to Nat Nakasa, 3 February 1963, Fol. B1, Nathaniel Nakasa Papers.
18 Nat Nakasa to Lewis Nkosi, 22 October 1963, Fol. B1, Nathaniel Nakasa Papers.
19 Nkosi, 'Review of *The World of Nat Nakasa*', 477.
20 Gordimer, 'One Man Living Through It', 10.
21 Nat Nakasa to Lewis Nkosi, 29 May 1963, Fol. B1, Nathaniel Nakasa Papers.
22 Can Themba to Nat Nakasa, 15 June 1963, Fol. B1, Nathaniel Nakasa Papers.
23 Arthur Maimane to Nat Nakasa, 15 September 1963, Fol. B1, Nathaniel Nakasa Papers.
24 Joe Thloloe, interview with the author, Johannesburg, November 2011.
25 Nat Nakasa to Lewis Nkosi, 29 May 1963, Fol. B1, Nathaniel Nakasa Papers; Nakasa, 'Comment', 4; Es'kia Mphahlele to Nat Nakasa, 28 June 1963, Fol. B1, Nathaniel Nakasa Papers.
26 John Thompson to Nat Nakasa, 7 June 1963, Fol. B3, Nathaniel Nakasa Papers ; Nat Nakasa to Lewis Nkosi, 22 October 1963, Fol. B1, Nathaniel Nakasa Papers; Gordimer, 'One Man Living Through It', 10.
27 Nakasa, 'Comment', 4.
28 John Thompson to Nat Nakasa, 13 August 1963, Fol. B3, Nathaniel Nakasa Papers.
29 For more on the role of small literary magazines in advancing South African literature during the 1960s, see Leger, 'Rediscovering *The Classic*'.
30 Mongane Serote, interview with the author, Braamfontein, Johannesburg, November 2011.
31 Barney Simon, 'My Years with "The Classic": A Note', *English in Africa* 7:2 (September 1980), 79.
32 Nat Nakasa to Arthur Maimane, 28 June 1963, Fol. B1, Nathaniel Nakasa Papers; Simon, 'My Years with "The Classic"', 76.
33 Barney Simon, 'Epilogue', in Dugmore Boetie, *Familiarity is the Kingdom of the Lost* (New York: Four Walls Eight Windows, 1989), 163.

34 Nat Nakasa to Ezekiel Mphahlele, 18 November 1963, Fol. B1, Nathaniel Nakasa Papers.

35 Margreet de Lange, *The Muzzled Muse: Literature and Censorship in South Africa* (Amsterdam: John Benjamins, 1991), 20.

36 'Censorship in South Africa. Beacon for Freedom', accessed 13 September 2010, http://www.beaconforfreedom.org/about_database/south%20africa.html.

37 Ehmeir, 'Publishing South African Litreature', 122.

38 Martin Meredith, *Mandela: A Biography* (New York: Public Affairs, 1997), 270–7; Nelson Mandela, *Long Walk to Freedom: The Autobiography of Nelson Mandela* (New York: Little, Brown, 1994), 375.

39 Paton had been stripped of his passport in 1960 upon returning from a trip to the United States to receive an award called the New York Freedom medal. As he explained to a reporter, 'I interpret this summary withdrawal of my passport as being the penalty after 12 years of Nationalist rule for continuing to say and write what I think to be the truth.' See Shapiro, 'No Exit?', 5.

40 Can Themba, 'The Bottom of the Bottle', *The Will to Die*, 112.

41 Nat Nakasa to R.T.B. Butlin, 24 July 1963, Fol. B3, Nathaniel Nakasa Papers; Nat Nakasa to R.T.B. Butlin, 9 September 1963, Fol. B3, Nathaniel Nakasa Papers: Nat Nakasa to 'The Public Affairs Officer, American Embassy', 4 December 1963, Fol. B3, Nathaniel Nakasa Papers.

42 Anthony Schulter to Nat Nakasa, 16 September 1963, Fol. B3, Nathaniel Nakasa Papers.

43 Helen Suzman to Louis Lyons, 7 February 1964, Folder Mb 2.3.1, Helen Suzman Papers, University of the Witwatersrand, Historical Papers.

44 Acott, 'Tactics of the Habitat', 9; Allister Sparks, interview, *Nat Nakasa: A Native of Nowhere*.

45 Roseinnes Phahle, interview with the author, Killarney, Johannesburg, 1 August 2012.
46 Nat Nakasa, 'A Labour Crisis', *Rand Daily Mail*, 14 March 1964, 5.
47 Nat Nakasa, 'The Hazards of Too Much Education', *Rand Daily Mail*, 16 May 1964, 11.
48 Nat Nakasa, 'Johannesburg: The City with Two Faces', *Rand Daily Mail*, 21 March 1964, 10.
49 Nat Nakasa, 'Meeting the New MPs', *The World of Nat Nakasa*, 64.
50 Hugh Masekela, interview with the author, Chapel Hill, NC, 12 October 2010.
51 Nat Nakasa, 'Living with My Private Thoughts', *Rand Daily Mail*, 30 May 1964, 11.
52 '8 Newspapermen Are Selected as Nieman Fellows at Harvard', *New York Times*, 4 June 1964, 27.
53 Nat Nakasa, 'Castles in the Air', *The Classic* 2:1 (1966): 25; Pippa Green, 'Nat Nakasa, Symbol of Exile's Loneliness', *Sunday Independent*, 17 July 1999, accessed 15 April 2010, http://www.iol.co.za/index.php?set_id.
54 Shapiro, 'No Exit?', 4.
55 Thanks to Karin Shapiro for alerting me to the existence of these records. National Archives, Pretoria, BAO 3610: C100/6/2460, Paspoort Todd and Esme Matshikiza; BAO 3610: C100/6/2461 Paspoort Miriam Makeba; BAO 3471: C100/6/658 Paspoort Barbara Hugh; NTS 2752: 1155/301 Paspoort William Modisane; BAO 3563: C100/6/1813 Paspoort Sheila Cingo; NTS 2769: 1623/301 Paspoort Lewis Nkosi; Marion Scher, 'What I've Learnt: Hugh Masekela', *Times Live*, 30 October 2011, accessed 20 November 2011, http://www.timeslive.co.za/lifestyle/2011/10/30/what-i-ve-learnt-hugh-Hugh.
56 Roseinnes Phahle, interview with the author, Killarney, Johannesburg, 1 August 2012.

57 National Archives, Pretoria, BAO 3561: C100/6/1789, Paspoort Nathaniel Nakasa, 11.
58 Nat Nakasa to John Thompson, 20 July 1964, Box 76, Fol. 4, International Association for Cultural Freedom Papers, University of Chicago.
59 Gordimer, 'One Man Living Through It', 12.
60 Nat Nakasa, 'Trying to Avoid Bitterness', *The Classic* 2:1 (1966), 70.
61 National Archives, Pretoria, BAO 3563: C100/6/1813 Paspoort Sheila Cingo.
62 Ross, *A Concise History of South Africa*, 146.
63 Department of Justice file for Nathaniel Nakasa, 1959–1965, 17.
64 Ibid., 4.
65 Ibid., 9.
66 Nat Nakasa to John Thompson, 20 July 1964, Box 76, Fol. 4, International Association for Cultural Freedom Papers.
67 Nat Nakasa, 'A Native of Nowhere', *Rand Daily Mail*, 19 September 1964, 9.
68 'S.A. Needs Nat Nakasa', *Rand Daily Mail*, 11 September 1964, 18.
69 Nadine Gordimer, telephone interview with the author, 4 November 2010.
70 David Hazelhurst, interview with the author, Johannesburg, November 2011; Allister Sparks, interview with the author, Rivonia, Johannesburg, 21 October 2011.
71 Memorandum on Nathaniel Nakasa, 28 April 1965, Federal Bureau of Investigation File on Nathaniel Nakasa. In possession of author.
72 Gordimer, 'One Man Living Through It', 15.
73 Nakasa, 'A Native of Nowhere', 9.
74 Lewis moved to London upon completing his Nieman fellowship in 1962.
75 Modisane, *Blame Me on History*, 311.
76 Casey Motsisi, 'We Remember You All …!', *Drum*, March 1963, 15

Chapter 6

1 Parker Donham, 'Nieman Fellow Recalls Experiences with Malcolm X', *Harvard Crimson*, 24 February 1965, accessed 24 January 2011, http://www.thecrimson.com/article/1965/2/24/nieman-fellow-recalls-experiences-with-malcolm.
2 Hugh Masekela, interview with the author, Chapel Hill, NC, 12 October 2010.
3 Kathleen Conwell, 'Letter to Nat Nakasa', *The World of Nat Nakasa*, xxxiv.
4 Hugh Masekela, interview with the author, Chapel Hill, NC, 12 October 2010.
5 Esmé Matshikiza, telephone interview with the author, 26 May 2012.
6 Special Agent in Charge (SAC) to Director, FBI, 14 June 1965, Federal Bureau of Investigation File on Nathaniel Nakasa.
7 Shortly thereafter, Tanganyika, which had by then been independent for three years, joined with the island of Zanzibar to become the United Republic of Tanzania.
8 Nakasa, 'A Native of Nowhere', 9.
9 Memorandum on Nathaniel Nakasa, 28 April 1965, Federal Bureau of Investigation File on Nathaniel Nakasa.
10 Nat Nakasa, 'Met with Smiles and Questions', *Rand Daily Mail*, 28 November 1964, 11.
11 Memorandum on Nathaniel Nakasa, 28 April 1965, Federal Bureau of Investigation File on Nathaniel Nakasa.
12 Nakasa, 'Met with Smiles and Questions', 11.
13 Ibid.

Chapter 7

1 Nakasa, 'Met with Smiles and Questions', 11.
2 Exchange Visitor Visa Application, INS File A13-968-005: Nathaniel Nakasa, United States Bureau of Citizenship and Immigration Services. In possession of author.

3 Fellow Nieman Ray Jenkins provided the characterisation of Nat as 'shy and reticent'. Several others, including Nieman Tim Creer and former Harvard/Radcliffe students Gail Gerhart, Jennifer Leaning and Parker Donham, similarly remembered him as a vague presence, someone they encountered on campus, but didn't know well. Ray Jenkins, telephone interview with author, 28 February 2011; Gail Gerhart, email message to author, 15 March 2011; Jennifer Leaning, email message to author, 31 March 2011; Tim Creery, email message to author, 19 June 2010; Parker Donham, email message to author, 10 March 2011.
4 Hugh Masekela, interview with the author, Chapel Hill, NC, 12 October 2010.
5 'About Nat Nakasa', The South African National Editors' Forum, accessed 1 March 2011, http://www.sanef.org.za/awards/about_the_nat_Nat_award.
6 Es'kia Mphahlele, 'Africa in Exile', *Daedalus* 111:2 (1982), 46.
7 Chinua Achebe, *Home and Exile* (Oxford: Oxford University Press, 2000), 92–3.
8 The term 'newsmen' is an accurate summary of not only all of the Nieman fellows in Nat's class, but of nearly all of those who completed the programme in that era more generally. From the approximately 180 Nieman fellows selected in the decade of the 1960s, exactly four were women. See 'Meet the Fellows: Alumni Fellows', The Nieman Foundation, accessed 12 April 2011, http://www.nieman.harvard.edu/NiemanFoundation/NiemanFellowships/MeetTheFellows/AlumniFellows.aspx.
9 Ray Jenkins, telephone interview with the author, 28 February 2011.
10 Quoted in John Gerhart, 'Silhouette: Nathaniel Nakasa', *Harvard Crimson*, 31 March 1965, accessed 14 February 2011, http://www.thecrimson.com/article/1965/3/31/nathaniel-Nat-pthe-first-time-i.
11 Quoted in John Bethell, *Harvard Observed: An Illustrated History of the University in the Twentieth Century* (Cambridge: Harvard University Press, 1998), 219.

12 Andrew Schlesinger, *Veritas: Harvard College and the American Experience* (Chicago: Ivan Dee, 2005), 221.
13 Harold McDougall, 'Negro Students' Challenge to Liberalism', *Harvard Crimson*, 31 May 1967, accessed 9 April 2011, http://www.thecrimson.com/article/1967/5/31/negro-students-challenge-to-liberalism-pthe.
14 Participation in SDS certainly was not limited to men, but Harvard women who joined the group were students at the all-female college of the University, Radcliffe, which had separate single-sex dorms elsewhere in Cambridge, so they would not have lived in Adams.
15 Ray Jenkins, telephone interview with the author, 28 February 2011.
16 Ray Jenkins, 'Memories of Nat Nakasa' (Unpublished manuscript, 1965.) In possession of author.
17 Harold McDougall, 'To Nat', *Harvard Yearbook* (Cambridge: Harvard University, 1966), 130.
18 Nakasa, 'Met with Smiles and Questions', 11.
19 Ronald Formisano, *Boston Against Busing: Race, Class, and Ethnicity in the 1960s and 1970s* (Chapel Hill: University of North Carolina Press, 2003), 25.
20 Mphahlele, 'Africa in Exile', 47; McDougall, 'To Nat', 130.
21 N.E. Sonderling, 'Nathaniel Ndazana Nakasa', *New Dictionary of South African Biography* (Pretoria: Vista), 1999.
22 Gail Gerhart, email message to author, 15 March 2011. Gerhart was herself a Radcliffe student in 1964/5, and the student she referenced dating Nat Nakasa was a friend and fellow student named Jennifer Leaning.
23 Ray Jenkins, telephone interview with the author, 28 February 2011.
24 Alan Venable, telephone interview with the author, 10 July 2010.
25 Jenkins, 'Memories of Nat Nakasa'.
26 Ibid.
27 Thomas Pettigrew, interview with Alan Venable, 10 October 1970. Notes in possession of author.
28 Jenkins, 'Memories of Nat Nakasa'.

29 Ray Jenkins, telephone interview with the author, 28 February 2011.
30 Nat Nakasa, 'Mr. Nakasa Goes to Harlem', *New York Times Magazine*, 7 February 1965, 40.
31 Harold wrote, 'a Harlem bookstore owner showed him a picture of the body of a Negro man in flames. Whites stood in the photograph laughing – men, women, children.' See McDougall, 'To Nat', 130. A reporter for the *Harvard Crimson*, John Gerhart, also described the photo, 'the burned body of a Negro lynch-victim lying on a pile of embers while a crowd of whites leered out of the darkness behind.' John Gerhart, 'Silhouette: Nat Nakasa', *Harvard Crimson*, 31 March 1965.
32 Nakasa, 'Mr. Nakasa Goes to Harlem', 40, 48.
33 While in Harlem, Nat also went looking for his one-time companion in Dar es Salaam, Malcolm X, who kept an office in the stately Hotel Theresa, a neighbourhood institution that housed many black luminaries passing through New York City. But after several visits, they still hadn't crossed paths, and Nat reluctantly gave up. When the writer returned to Harvard, however, Brother Malcolm followed. On 16 December 1964, the former Nation of Islam leader gave a speech at the Harvard Law School entitled 'The African Revolution and its Impact on the American Negro'. There is no direct indication that Nat was there that night, but given his history with Malcolm X and his interest in the subject matter at hand, it seems highly likely that he would have attended. And as a black writer thousands of miles from home, he may well have taken comfort in Malcolm X's assertion that 'We certainly can't hate Africa and at the same time learn to love ourselves.' See Malcolm X, 'The African Revolution and its Impact on the American Negro' (Speech given at the Harvard Law School Forum, Cambridge, Massachusetts, 16 December 1964), http://www.brothermalcolm.net/mxwords/whathesaid10.html; Nakasa, 'Mr. Nakasa Goes to Harlem', 41.
34 'Africa Symposium', *Harvard Crimson*, 16 April 1965, accessed 30April2010,http://theharvardcrimson.com/article/1965/4/16/africa-

symposium-pnathaniel-Nat-south-african.
35 Conwell, 'Letter to Nat Nakasa', xxxiii.
36 'South African Nieman Fellow Falls to Death', Undated clipping, INS File A13-968-005: Nathaniel Nakasa.
37 'Changing World, Essay 11: South Africa: One Nation, Two Nationalisms', National Education Television Network, 1965, WNET: New York Public Media.
38 INS File A13-968-005: Nathaniel Nakasa, 6; Memorandum on Nathaniel Nakasa, 28 April 1965, Federal Bureau of Investigation File on Nathaniel Nakasa.
39 Special Agent in Charge (SAC), Boston, to Director, FBI, 28 April 1965, Federal Bureau of Investigation File on Nathaniel Nakasa.
40 Peter Kihss, 'Malcolm X Shot to Death at Rally Here', *New York Times*, 22 February 1965, 1.
41 Parker Donham, 'Nieman Fellow Recalls Experiences with Malcolm X', *Harvard Crimson*. http://www.thecrimson.com/article/1965/2/24/nieman-fellow-recalls-experiences-with-malcolm.
42 Harry Mashabela, interview with the author, Pretoria, 10 February 2012.
43 For further detail on the origins and growth of the early anti-apartheid movement in the United States, see Francis Nesbitt, *Race for Sanctions: African Americans Against Apartheid, 1946–1994* (Bloomington: Indiana University Press, 2004).
44 'Action in Boston Against U.S. Partnership in Apartheid', Leaflet, March 1965. In possession of author.
45 'South Africa', *Harvard Crimson*, 16 March 1965, accessed 10 February 2011, http://theharvardcrimson.com/article/1965/3/16/south-africa-pthe-sds-will-sponsor.
46 'Pickets Censure Apartheid Policy,' *Harvard Crimson*, 20 March 1965, accessed 16 February 2011, http://www.thecrimson.com/article/1965/3/20/pickets-censure-apartheid-policy-pover-100.
47 Ibid.
48 Program, National Conference on South African Crisis and American

Action, 21–23 March 1965, accessed 10 April 2011, http://bit.ly/i24ILW.

49 Harvard student activist Alan Venable, who was in the audience that day, remembers the speech being not so much incendiary as simply despairing and relentlessly negative about the situation in South Africa. Alan Venable, correspondence with the author, 15 July 2013.

50 Department of Justice file for Nathaniel Nakasa, 1958–1965, 1.

51 Special Agent in Charge (SAC), Boston, to Director, FBI, 28 April 1965, Federal Bureau of Investigation File on Nathaniel Nakasa.

52 John Gerhart, 'Silhouette: Nathaniel Nakasa'.

53 Peter Magubane, interview with the author, Johannesburg, 24 July 2012; Memorandum on Nathaniel Nakasa, 28 April 1965, Federal Bureau of Investigation File on Nathaniel Nakasa.

54 Allister Sparks, interview, *Nat Nakasa: A Native of Nowhere*.

55 Conwell, 'Letter to Nat Nakasa', xxxiv.

56 Jenkins, 'Memories of Nat Nakasa'.

57 Hugh Masekela, interview with the author, Chapel Hill, NC, 12 October 2010.

58 Jenkins, 'Memories of Nat Nakasa'.

59 Ibid.

60 Green, 'Nat Nakasa, Symbol of Exile's Loneliness'.

61 Nakasa, 'Mr. Nakasa Goes to Harlem', 40.

62 Hugh Masekela, interview with the author, Chapel Hill, NC, 12 October 2010.

63 Nadine Gordimer, telephone interview with the author, 4 November 2010; Nadine Gordimer, personal interview with the author, 19 April 2012.

64 Allister Sparks, interview, *Nat Nakasa: A Native of Nowhere*.

65 Hugh remembers that the play was a new work by Lorraine Hansberry, the renowned writer of *A Raisin in the Sun*. However, Hansberry died in January 1965, the same night as her final play, *The Sign in Sidney Brustein's Window*, closed on Broadway. It is likely instead that the play they had tickets to was 'The Owl and the Pussycat', a comedic

Broadway show in which Sands was then starring at the American National Theater and Academy Theater on W. 52nd St. See the *New York Times* theatre listings for that weekend. 'Theater Directory', *New York Times*, 13 July 1965, 40; Hugh Masekela, interview with the author, Chapel Hill, NC, 12 October 2010.

66 New York Police Department File 2009PL2930, Nathaniel Nakasa (in possession of author); John Thompson, interview, *Nat Nakasa: A Native of Nowhere*; M.C. Blackman, 'Nathaniel Nakasa Will Be Buried in Alien Soil, Far from South Africa', *New York Herald Tribune*, 17 July 1965.

67 'Services are Held for African Writer', *New York Times*, 17 July 1965, 11.

68 Hugh Masekela, interview with the author, Chapel Hill, NC, 12 October 2010.

69 'Nat Nakasa buried near Malcolm X', *Ilanga lase Natal*, 24 July 1965, 2.

70 Athol Fugard, 'Letter from Athol Fugard', *The Classic* 2:1 (1966), 78.

71 Nakasa, 'Castles in the Air', 110.

72 Special Agent in Charge (SAC), Boston, to Director, FBI, 23 July 1965, Federal Bureau of Investigation File on Nathaniel Nakasa.

73 Willie Kgositsile, interview with the author, Johannesburg, 21 May 2012.

74 Gordimer, 'One Man Living Through It', 16.

75 Nakasa, 'Oh, to Be an Anonymous Houseboy', *The World of Nat Nakasa*, 61.

76 Simon, 'My Years with "The Classic"', 78.

77 Gordimer, 'One Man Living Through It', 16.

Conclusion

1 New York Police Department File 2009PL2930, Nathaniel Nakasa. In possession of the author.

2 Leslie Sehume, interview with the author, Dube, Soweto, 8 February

2012; Nadine Gordimer, interview with the author, Parktown, Johannesburg, 19 April 2012; Allister Sparks, interview with the author, Rivonia, Johannesburg, 21 October 2011.

3 Willie Kgositsile, interview with the author, Johannesburg, 21 May 2012.

4 Juby Mayet, interview with the author, Lenasia, 5 December 2011.

5 Alf Kumalo, interview with the author, Diepkloof, Soweto, 28 November 2011.

6 Why, for instance, did the CIA refuse to release Nat's surveillance file to me, instead writing opaquely that they could 'neither confirm nor deny the existence or nonexistence of records responsive to [my] request'. (However, the letter went on, should these records exist, they remain 'properly classified' as a matter of national security.) The agency also later rejected an appeal of their initial denial. Scott Koch, Acting Information and Privacy Coordinator (CIA), to Ryan Brown, 1 September 2010. In possession of author.

7 'Letter to the Editor', *Ilanga lase Natal*, 24 July 1965.

8 Although Nakasa himself was never as widely known as some of his *Drum* compatriots in South Africa, a series of journalists became interested in his legacy in the course of the 1990s, and wrote pieces on his life and death. SANEF likely drew upon that budding public interest in choosing to name their award after Nakasa. For further detail about the Nakasa Award, as well as a list of winners, see 'Awards', South African National Editors' Forum, accessed 3 April 2011, http://www.sanef.org.za/awards. For journalistic pieces written on Nakasa in the early 1990s, see Dana Snyman, 'Nat Nakasa in Ongemerkte Graf in New York' [Nat Nakasa in Unmarked Grave in New York], *Beeld*, 1 September 1993, accessed 19 April 2011, http://152.111.1.88/argief/berigte/beeld/1993/09/1/8/11.html; Lewis Clapp, 'Will Nat Nakasa Ever Go Home?' *Nieman Notes*, 22 December 1993.

9 Jacob Zuma, Address at the SANEF Awards Dinner, South African Government Information, 30 June 2009, accessed 1 April 2011, http://www.info.gov.za/speech/DynamicAction?pageid=461&sid=7

80&tid=799.
10 'Discussion Document: Media Diversity and Ownership', African National Congress, 29 July 2010, accessed 1 April 2011, http://www.anc.org.za/docs/discus/2010/mediad.pdf.
11 Jeff Radebe, Speech at the 2010 SANEF Awards Dinner, Politics Web, 26 July 2010, accessed 4 April 2011, http://bit.ly/g7EXlJ.
12 Peter McDonald, 'The Present is Another Country', LitNet, 13 September 2010, accessed 4 April 2011, http://bit.ly/hciaOb.
13 Green, 'Nat Nakasa, Symbol of Exile's Loneliness'.
14 Nat Nakasa, 'On Writing in South Africa', *The World of Nat Nakasa*, 86.

Acknowledgements

This little book is like a glacier – you're seeing only the tiny fraction bobbing above the surface. Below is a vast network of people and institutions that have kept me afloat over the last three years; without them this project would never have taken the shape it did.

It's fair to say this book was born on a blustery January morning in Durham, North Carolina, when I walked out of a seminar room at Duke University after the first day of a course on South African history, determined that I was going to find a way to impress the incisive, brilliant professor who'd led the class that day. Soon, in a flailing attempt to do just that, I was spending my nights in the library thumbing through old issues of a glossy South African magazine called *Drum*, looking for articles by a man named Nat Nakasa. A year later, I'd finished an undergraduate honours thesis about Nat and was headed to South Africa to continue studying his life. So I believe it's accurate to argue that this book owes its very existence to that professor, Karin Shapiro, who has been both a mentor and dear friend to me over the past few years, and to whom I owe more than I could ever say.

During my time as a student at Duke University, Karin was joined in cheerleading and cajoling me into finishing this project by a small army of other historians and historians-in-training. In particular I would like to thank Rose Filler, Karlyn Forner and Andrew Walker, who have – essentially against their will – become Nat Nakasa experts over the past three years. I owe a great deal to both their academic guidance and their fierce emotional support. Additionally, thanks to Professor Janet Ewald, Brooke Hartley, Alyssa Granacki, Snayha Nath and the entire cadre of history students who slogged through their own thesis projects alongside me in 2010–11. All of you may still be wondering what became of the year of your lives that dropped into a black hole known as 'thesis writing', but know that it could be much worse. I've lost nearly three.

After I graduated from Duke, the continuation of my research on Nat's life was funded by a fellowship from the US Department of State's Fulbright programme, which allowed me the almost unbelievable luxury of spending a year living in Johannesburg and putting together this manuscript. There I frequently found the line between research informant and friend blurred, as archivists, interview subjects and professors took me under their wing, helping this new South African transplant navigate everything from archive visits to buying a car and braaiing my first boerewors. In particular, Gail Gerhart pointed me to sources, connected me to archives and interviews, and then, as if that were not enough, rented me her flat. Meanwhile, Heather and Mike Acott, Tessa and Govin

Reddy, and Louise Colvin generously welcomed me into their homes, lives and conversations. Heather in particular kept an eye on me and my rickety old Toyota Corolla as we crisscrossed South Africa that year, always waiting in the wings with a spot at her dinner table and an idea for a book I should read. At the same time, the students and staff of the history department at the University of the Witwatersrand warmly welcomed me into their fold; particular thanks are due to professors Clive Glaser and Phil Bonner for allowing me to join the club.

A wide variety of institutions opened their arms to my research project, and I would like to thank the dedicated staffs of the University of the Witwatersrand Historical Papers collection, the South African History Archive, the Killie Campbell Africana Library, the University of Durban-Westville's Gandhi Luthuli Documentation Centre, the National English Literary Museum, Bailey's African History Archive, the National Library of South Africa, and the South Africa National Archives, as well as the librarians at the University of the Witwatersrand's Cullen Library and the libraries of the University of South Africa. Particular thanks are due to Mwelela Cele at Killie Campbell and Crystal Warren at NELM for the specific interest and enthusiasm they took in my research.

Liz Gunner, Jon Soske and Christopher Lee gave early votes of confidence to my research on Nat by publishing it in academic journals, while Liz, Abdul Bemath, Lindy Stiebel and Michael Chapman lent me their vast bibliographic knowledge of South African literature. Kate Ryan, Vusi Kumalo and Sanele Garane all did translation work for me.

Meanwhile, over the course of my research I was lucky enough to meet four other people working on projects with subjects relating to Nat Nakasa – Margot Leger, Emily Gall, Matthew Keaney and Alan Venable. All of them staggered me by their generosity with both their time and their sources, reminding me that history is always a collaborative effort. Indeed, my research stands on the shoulders of theirs, and I am forever indebted to the foundation they laid for me.

One of the greatest joys of this project was sitting face to face with those who knew Nat during his short life. Without exception they were generous with their time, memories and tea. Among them were a large number of journalists, all of them cutting, acerbic and deeply intelligent observers of South African society past and present, who reminded me at a crucial life juncture just why this profession is so valuable to the world. I wish I could thank them all individually for their great insight and generosity towards this young writer. My deepest gratitude is due, in no particular order, to Hugh Masekela, Nadine Gordimer, Alf Kumalo, Allister Sparks, Barbara Bailey, Caiphus Semenya, David Hazelhurst, Enoch Duma, Esmé Matshikiza, Frances Jowell (Suzman), Harry Mashabela, Joe Thloloe, Juby Mayet, Ken Carstens, Leslie Sehume, Peter Magubane, Ranjith Kally, Roseinnes Phahle, Mongane Wally Serote, Willy Kgositsile, Dunbar Moodie, Abraham Mashugane, Michael Gardiner, Philip Kgosana, Oswald Mtshali, Tim Creery, Parker Donham, Ray Jenkins and Jennifer Leaning.

Of course, the people whose support has meant the absolute most during this research are the members of the Nakasa family, whose warm welcome and open hearts were more than I could have ever asked for. First and foremost, Nat's sister, Gladys Maphumulo, took a great interest in my project from the moment we first talked over a scratchy phone connection from North Carolina, and gave vastly of her time in helping me understand both Nat's early life and the history of their family. She welcomed me warmly into her home and her past, and gave me permission to quote from Nat's works in this text, for which I will be eternally grateful. Meanwhile, Nat's nieces and nephews Thami Nakasa, Nombulelo Nakasa, and Sipho Nakasa, as well as Jabu Mhlanga, drove me through Nat's old haunts, answered my questions, and asked many perceptive ones of their own. Their support of this book means more than they know.

There are not enough superlatives in the world for me to thank the people who have read this manuscript front-to-back and offered their commentary over its various iterations, but I will try. Karin, Jan, Gail, Heather, Alan, Karlyn, Rose and Jay: you are the best, greatest, loveliest and most beautiful people on this earth. Thank you. I also want to warmly thank Maggie Davey and Bridget Impey at Jacana Media for giving this book a home, and Kerrie Barlow and Russell Martin for their impeccable work in editing and organising the manuscript for publication.

The final debt I owe is to those who kept me (mostly) sane, well fed and laughing during the time I worked on this project: my dear friends and family. My parents, Beth Brown, Jay Brown and Allison Lee, and siblings, Joshua and Zoey Brown, have always been strangely encouraging of my tendency to disappear to far-flung corners of the world, and it is for them that I will always return home. Thank you to Sarah Goetz, Alex Oprea, Matthew Price, Hannah Thurman, Leo Brown, Heather Noble, Asya Pokrovskaya, Kara Miller, Vivienne Born and Allison Backman for their unflinching faith in me and this project over the years, which is undoubtedly the force that has shamed me into finishing this book. In Johannesburg, the Craighall Park Writers' Group kept me in wine and wisdom throughout the process, and it would be hard to envision better confidantes and southern Africa co-adventurers than the likes of Olivia Greene, Sarah Frostenson, Jenny Hoobler, Ryan Kilpatrick and the rest of the Fulbright crew. Finally, thanks to Anna Alcaro, and Micah Reddy for having the bravery (or, alternatively, the poor sense) to be my closest friends as I dove deep into this project. Without them – indeed, without everyone mentioned in the preceding pages – there would surely be no book in your hands today.

Ryan Lenora Brown
Boston, Massachusetts
5 August 2013

Index

Achebe, Chinua 134
African American 127, 132, 139, 142, 148, 155
African Drum, The 43
African National Congress (ANC) xvi, xviii, 22, 24, 42, 58, 59, 78, 80, 85, 107, 118, 150, 169, 170
Alabama 152, 153
Ann Arbor, Michigan 1
anti-apartheid x, 45, 47, 53, 78, 93, 94, 106, 107, 108, 109, 114, 122, 123, 148, 150, 171, 172
anti-pass campaigns 80
apartheid ix, x, xi–xiv, xvi–xviii, 3, 5, 6, 17, 25, 29, 34, 35, 37, 39, 40, 41, 46, 54, 58, 63–69, 71, 72, 74, 78–82, 87, 89, 93, 103, 108–112, 116–120, 122, 123, 124, 131–135, 142, 143, 147–151, 157, 158, 160, 162, 166

Argus Printing and Publishing 31
Awori, Aggrey 149

Bailey, Barbara 73
Bailey, Jim 43, 62, 73, 84, 85, 8
Bailey, Sir Abe 43
Baldwin, James 157
Ball State University, Indiana 117
banning orders 116, 119
Bantu Affairs Commissioner 116
Bantu Education Act 25, 59
Bantu Press 31
Basutoland 80, 88, 89
Bechuanaland 69, 70
Biko, Steve xiii, 172
Boetie, Dugmore 105
Boston 135, 138, 139, 145, 146, 149, 150, 159
Boston Globe 135
Botswana 69, 124, 167

British Broadcasting Corporation (BBC) 120

Cambridge, Massachusetts 116, 128, 137, 138, 139, 144, 151, 152, 154, 161
Cambridge, U.K. 160
Canada 153
Cape Times 23
Cape Town 69, 70, 88, 93, 107, 112, 114, 162
Cassire, Reinholt 72
Cato, George Christopher 8
Chesterville Cultural Club 30
Censorship 92, 93, 96, 106, 170
Central Intelligence Agency (CIA) 94, 97, 123, 168
Central Park ix, 154, 156, 164
civil rights 113, 127, 132, 137, 138, 140, 144, 146, 150, 152, 153
Classic, The 92, 93, 94, 95, 96, 97, 99, 100–105, 108, 134, 154, 161, 162
Cold War 94, 97
Cole, Ernest 45
colour line 39, 54, 69, 71, 92, 162
communism 46, 93, 94, 97, 98, 119, 123, 148
communist 56, 93, 94, 98, 118, 123, 163
Communist Party 46
Coney Island 73

Congo 160
Congress for Racial Equality 149
Contrast 102
Conwell, Kathleen 144, 152
Crescent Restaurant 56

Damons, Leroy 70
Damons, Maud 69, 70, 71
Dar es Salaam 126, 128, 129, 146, 160
Day, Noel 149
Departure from the Union Regulation Act 1955 82
democratic election 1994
detention 120
Dhlomo, Herbert 32
District Six, Cape Town 42
Dlamini, Jacob xiii
Drum xiv, 32, 34, 35, 37, 43–54, 57, 58, 62, 63, 64, 66–69, 71, 73, 80, 82–87, 89, 91, 93, 95, 96, 99, 100, 102, 103, 109, 114, 116, 117, 118, 120, 121, 124, 128, 134, 142, 145, 153, 157, 163, 166, 168
Dube, John 31
Duma, Enoch 29, 30, 60, 62
Duma, William 16
Durban xi, xii, xiii, 1, 5–12, 21, 23, 26, 27, 28, 30–34, 37, 41, 48, 49, 116, 140, 157, 169

Cato Manor 8, 16, 17, 19, 21, 22, 36, 42, 121, 162
Chesterville 1, 9, 11, 15, 21, 30
Chili's tearoom 10
Grey Street 19, 20
Luthuli's tearoom 10
Victoria Street 10
Warwick Avenue 20

Eastern Bloc 97
editorial freedom 6, 32
Eisenhower, Dwight 38
Elangeni Hotel 169
election 1948 17, 18, 19, 172
Empire State Building ix
England *see* United Kingdom
Eshowe High School 25, 26, 34
Esquire 153
exile x, xii, xviii, 40, 80, 83, 88, 93, 96, 101, 107, 108, 116, 117, 122, 124, 130, 133, 134, 139, 145, 150, 153, 157, 158, 160, 162, 163, 165, 166, 167, 171
exit permit ix, 82, 113, 114, 116, 119, 121, 128

Faneuil Hall 149
Farfield Foundation 81, 97, 98, 99, 102, 168
Farmer, James 150
Federal Bureau of Investigation (FBI) 133, 146, 151, 158, 159
Ferncliff Cemetery 157

First National Bank of Boston 149
forced removals 63, 118
Fordsburg 56, 57
France 124, 160
Francophone Africa 102
Frank Campbell Funeral Home 156
freedom movement xvi, 149
fringe county 39, 40, 54, 81, 83, 105, 117, 123, 155, 161, 163, 172
Fugard, Athol 102, 158
Fulbright fellowship (programme) 117, 203, 207

Ghana 44, 81, 84, 112
Glasser, Spike 69, 70, 71
Goa Island 88
Golden City Post 44
Gordimer, Nadine 64, 72, 73, 91, 100, 101, 102, 109, 116, 120, 121, 155, 159, 161, 163
Great Depression 31
Green, Pippa 171
Greenwich Village 130
Group Areas Act 1950 41

Harlem 142, 143, 144, 152, 154, 155, 156, 164
Harlem Renaissance 46
Harvard Crimson 135, 147, 151
Harvard
    Adams House 136, 137

East African Students' Organisation 149
Radcliffe 136, 139
Square 136, 153
University ix, 81, 95, 108, 113, 131, 135–138, 140, 142, 144, 146, 149, 154, 161, 165, 173
Widener Library 135
Yard 135, 149
Hazelhurst, David 57, 64, 120
Head, Bessie 117, 124
Hempstone, Smith 113
Herenigde Nasionale Party (Reunited National Party) 17
Highveld 41
homeland 3, 111, 112, 117, 145
homesickness 142, 153
Hong Kong 5
Hopkinson, Tom 83, 84
human rights 78, 127

Identity Document(ID) 28
Ilanga lase Natal 3, 12, 31, 32, 33, 34, 168
Immigration and Naturalization Services (INS) 133, 145, 146
Immorality Act 59, 69, 71
India 7, 113, 135
Indian Views 11, 24
Indiana 117
Information and Analysis: South Africa 101

intellectuals xvii, xviii, 39, 40–43, 54, 58, 65, 67, 68, 95, 98, 114, 116, 121, 124, 132, 173
international refugee 146
Iran 135
Ivy League x

Jackson, Shirley 106
  The Lottery 106
Jan Smuts International Airport 82, 121
Jenkins, Ray 113, 137, 140, 141, 153
Johannesburg xiv, xv, xvii, 4, 13, 16, 32, 34–43, 45, 48, 54–58, 61, 62, 67, 68, 70, 71, 72, 75, 77, 80–83, 86, 87, 89, 92, 95, 104, 106, 109, 111, 112, 116, 121, 126, 131, 134, 138, 142, 144, 145, 147, 151, 166
  Albert Street 52
  Eloff Street 51
  Frere Road 72
  Hilbrow 56, 60, 74
  Hyde Park 53
  Mooi Street 52
  Norwood 120
  Park Station 36, 41
  Parktown 100
  Yeoville 56
Jonker, Ingrid 102, 162, 163
Jowell, Fancie *see* Susman, Francie
journalists x, xi, xii, xvii, xviii, 2,

11, 37, 43, 52, 60, 67, 73, 81, 86, 92, 93, 108, 113, 135, 169, 170

Kenya 44, 113
Kgosana, Philip 88, 89, 90
Kgositsile, Willie 74, 159, 165
Knickerbocker Hospital 164
Kroonstad 117
Kumalo, Alf 70, 121, 160, 167
Kunene, Obed 26
KwaZulu-Natal 7

League of Nations 85
Lelyveld, Joseph xvii
Lenox Avenue, Harlem 154
Lesotho 80
Lessing, Doris 104
Liberal Party 108
Liberia 160
Lilliesleaf farm 106
Lobatse 69
London 5, 96, 125, 128, 129, 134, 159, 165
Los Angeles Times 23, 135
Lusaka 121, 128
Lusophone Africa 102
Luthuli, Albert 78
Luthuli's tearoom 10

Madondo, George 19
Magubane, Peter 45, 49, 69, 71, 85, 86, 87, 88, 89, 152

Maimane, Arthur 80, 96, 101
Makeba, Miriam 114, 130, 154, 155, 157, 159, 160
Malan, Rev Dr D.F. 17, 18
Manchester 5
Mandela, Nelson xiii, xv, xvii, 74, 107, 116, 171
Mandela, Winnie xix, 74
Manhattan 130, 142, 146
Maphumulo, Gladys *see* Nakasa, Gladys
March 1960 protests 77, 83, 84
Marshall Square 51
Marshall, Lawrence 150
Marxist 82
  literature 46
  principles 93
Masekela, Barbara 114, 154
Masekela, Hugh x, xiii, 114, 127, 130, 133, 153, 154, 155, 157, 159, 165
Maseru 89
Mashabela, Harry 58, 147
mass removals 36, 62
Massachusetts League of Woman Voters 144
Matshikiza, Todd 45, 80, 114, 124, 128, 163
Mayet, Juby 52, 53, 59, 74, 166
Mbeki, Thabo xv, xvi, xvii, 58, 59
McDonald, Peter 170
McDougall, Harold 137, 139, 140, 143

Meer, Ismail 11
mental asylum 6
hospital xiv, 16
   illness xiii, 3, 15, 155, 156
missionary education 3, 25, 126
Mkele, Nimrod 154
Modisane, Bloke 42, 68, 80, 114, 124
Montgomery Advertiser 113, 140
Monro, John 136
Motlanthe, Kgalema xv
Motsisi, Casey 101, 114, 124, 125
Mozambique 88
Mphahlele, Es'kia 101, 114, 124, 134, 139
multiracial parties xi, 39, 83, 131

Nabokov, Vladimir 106
   Lolita 106
Nakasa, Alvina 7, 10, 11, 15, 16, 17, 158
Nakasa, Chamberlain 2, 3, 7, 10, 11, 12, 13, 14, 15, 16, 21, 24, 25, 27, 157
   Ivangeli Lokuz' Akha or *The Gospel of Self Help* 13
Nakasa, Gladys (Maphumulo) xii, 1, 2, 3, 4, 15, 17, 21, 167
Nakasa, Mabel 1
Nakasa, Moses 3, 11, 15, 156, 160, 165, 167

Nakasa, Nathaniel Ndazana (Nat)
   birth and childhood 11, 15–16, 24
   schooling 25–26
   reporter on *Ilanga lase Natal* 31–34
   appointment to *Drum* 34–37
   move to Johannesburg 35–37
   working for *Drum* 43–90
   founding and editing of *The Classic* 91–108
   writing for *Rand Daily Mail* 109–113
   awarded Nieman fellowship 113–116
   decision to go into exile 113–125
   stayover in Dar es Salaam 126–128
   arrival in US 129–130
   fellowship at Harvard 131–154
   visit to Harlem 142–144, 154–155
   death and funeral 156–158, 164–169
Namibia *see also* South West Africa 85
Nat Nakasa Award 169
Natal Indian Congress 22
Natal Mercury 23
Nation of Islam 146
National Education Television Network 144

National Party (NP) 5, 18, 19, 24,
    28, 36, 40, 41, 60, 79, 85, 87,
    93, 94, 105, 106, 110, 111, 117,
    122, 145, 148, 163, 172
New African, The 106
New Age 52
New Jersey 159
New York x, 129, 130, 150, 153,
    155, 157, 162, 165
New York Times x, xvii, 5, 79, 83,
    109, 133, 135, 142, 143, 144,
    152
Nicholson, Ann 59
Nigeria 44, 134
Nkosi, Lewis 26, 29–32, 38, 41,
    45, 48, 50, 53, 56, 60, 61, 62,
    71, 81, 82, 83, 95, 99, 101, 108,
    113, 114, 120, 122, 124
Nkrumah, President Kwame 112
Nokwe, Duma 58
Northern Rhodesia *see also*
    Zambia 121, 124
Nxumalo, Henry 45, 54

Observer, The 18
Orange Free State 117
Organisation of African Unity xvi
Orlando West 74, 75, 114
Oxford 43, 159, 160, 170

Pan African Congress (PAC) 78,
    85, 107, 160
pan-Africanism 126, 146

Paris 101
pass laws 28, 59, 77
passport 90, 108, 111, 113, 114,
    115, 117, 119, 120, 128, 160
Paton, Alan 13, 91, 107, 108
    Cry, the Beloved Country 13
Pettigrew, Thomas 140, 141
Phahle, Roseinnes 72, 110, 111,
    112, 114, 115
Pienaar, G.D. 77
Pollock, Jackson 97
Pondoland 85
Population Registration Act, 1950
    27
Princeton 147
Publications and Entertainment Act
    106
Purple Renoster, The (The Purple
    Rhinoceros) 102

Radcliffe 136, 139
Radebe, Jeff 170
race riot (Durban) 20, 21, 22, 23,
    24
Rand Daily Mail 52, 55, 58, 61,
    82, 95, 109, 110, 112, 113, 117,
    119, 120, 121, 122, 128–131,
    133, 152
Ray Street, Sophiatown 48
reference book 27, 28, 77, 111
residential segregation 57, 60, 138
Reuther, Victor 150
Rive, Richard 101

Rivonia 106, 107, 108
Robben Island 107, 116

Sampson, Anthony 43, 69
sanctions 148
Sands, Diana 155
Sarda, Shankar 113
Sehume, Leslie 51, 56, 64
Semenya, Caiphus 154
Senegal 98
Senghor, Léopold 98, 104
Serote, Mongane Wally 47, 65, 103, 104
Sharpeville 77, 78, 79, 80, 83, 84, 88, 93, 108, 132
   massacre 148
shebeen 30, 42, 44, 50, 51, 53, 64, 73, 81, 91, 96, 121, 135, 142
   Aunt Suzie's 51
   Church bar 52
   Classic bar 52, 91, 95
   Whitey's bar 51
Sierra Leone 44
Simon & Schuster 108
Simon, Barney 102, 104, 105
Sisulu, Walter 116
Smuts, Jan 18
Sobukwe, Robert 107
Sondlo, Victor 74
Sophiatown 41, 42, 43, 52, 62, 64, 72, 83, 121, 132, 142
South African Indian Congress 24

South African National Editors' Forum (SANEF) 169, 170
South Korea 135
South West Africa *see also* Namibia 85, 86, 87
Southern Rhodesia *see also* Zambia 84
Soviet Union 98
Soweto 58, 60, 64, 74, 75, 81, 83, 96, 121, 143
Sparks, Allister 109, 110, 120, 121, 132, 152, 155
Star, The 61
State of Emergency 78, 80, 84
Stravinsky, Igor 98
   Rite of Spring 98
Stein, Gertrude 135
Stein, Sylvester 34, 35, 43, 48, 80
Sterkfontein Mental Hospital 16
Stillman, Nat 147, 148, 149
Student Nonviolent Coordinating Committee 149
Students for a Democratic Society (SDS) 137, 148, 149, 150
Suppression of Communism Act 1950 46, 47, 59, 69, 93, 106, 119
Sussens, Aubrey 82
Suzman, Francie (Jowell) 53, 56, 57, 73, 81, 82, 159, 160
Suzman, Helen 53, 109
Swaziland 108, 124, 163

215

Tambo, Oliver xiii, 150
Tanganyika (Tanzania) 84, 126, 153
Themba, Can 45, 48, 49, 50, 52, 54, 71, 91, 101, 108, 116, 124, 163
Thloloe, Joe 44, 49, 52, 64, 101
Thompson, Jack 81, 96, 97, 98, 99, 103, 116, 119, 154, 156, 164, 168
Time 43
Transkei 111, 117, 145
Transkei Legislative Assembly 112
Tutu, Desmond 171

Uganda 149
Umgeni Road Baptist Church 16
Umlazi 4
UN Committee on South West Africa 86
underground 45, 78, 93, 122, 163
Union of South Africa 46, 47
United Kingdom (UK) 70, 90, 120, 124, 145, 156, 167, 115, 159
United Nations (UN) 78, 86, 148
United Party (UP) 17, 18, 24
United States (US) ix, x, 45, 82, 83, 94, 95, 96, 98, 108, 113, 114, 119, 121, 123, 124, 125, 127–130, 132, 133, 134, 138, 139, 144–149
University of North Carolina xiii
University of the Witwatersrand 56, 57, 72, 104
Urban Areas Act 1923 42

Verwoerd, Hendrik 25
Vorster, B.J. 119

Walker, Dick 85, 86
Warwick Avenue, Durban 20
Washington D.C. 128, 150, 151, 152
Washington, Booker T. 12
White House 148
Wolpe, Harold 82
World War I 85
World War II 5, 17

X, Malcolm 126, 127, 129, 146, 154, 157
Xuma, A.B. 42

Zambia *see also* Northern Rhodesia 121, 128, 163, 157
Zambia Broadcasting Corporation 128
Zindela, Theo 29, 30, 31, 70
Zululand 25
Zuma, Jacob xvi, xvii, 169